Psychoanalysis of Mythology

Cover image: Oedipus and the Sphinx, oil painting by Gustave Moreau, 1864.
Title page image: Oedipus dragging his father Laius from his chariot to kill him, marble relief from the 3rd century BC.

Psychoanalysis of Mythology

Freudian Theories on Myth and Religion Examined

Stefan Stenudd

Stefan Stenudd is a Swedish author, artist, and historian of ideas. He has published a number of books in Swedish as well as English, both fiction and non-fiction. Among the latter are books about mythology, Taoism, the cosmology of the Greek philosophers, the Japanese martial arts, Tarot, astrology, and life force concepts.

His novels explore existential subjects from Stone-Age drama to science fiction, but lately he focuses increasingly on the present.

In the history of ideas, he researches the thought patterns in creation myths, as well as theories about those myths through history.

He is also a 7 dan instructor in the peaceful martial art aikido, which he has practiced for 50 years.

He has his own extensive website: stenudd.com

Books by Stefan Stenudd:
Fake Lao Tzu Quotes: Erroneous Tao Te Ching Citations Examined, 2020.
Ever Young, 2017, 2018, 2020.
Sunday Brunch with the World Maker, 2016, 2018, 2020.
All's End, 2007, 2015.
Occasionally I Contemplate Murder, 2006, 2011, 2015.
Cosmos of the Ancients: The Greek Philosophers on Myth and Cosmology, 2007, 2011, 2015.
Tao Te Ching: The Taoism of Lao Tzu Explained, 2011, 2015.
Tao Quotes, 2013, 2015.
Tarot Unfolded: Imaginative Reading of the Divination Cards, 2012, 2015.
Life Energy Encyclopedia, 2009, 2015.
Qi: Increase Your Life Energy, 2008, 2009, 2015.
Aikido Principles, 2008, 2016.
Attacks in Aikido, 2008, 2009, 2015.
Aikibatto: Sword Exercises for Aikido Students, 2007, 2009.
Your Health in Your Horoscope: Introduction to Medical Astrology, 2009, 2015.

Psychoanalysis of Mythology:
Freudian Theories on Myth and Religion Examined.
© Stefan Stenudd, 2022. All rights reserved.
Book design by the author.
Publisher: Arriba, Malmö, Sweden, arriba.se
Hardcover edition
ISBN 978-91-7894-001-1

Contents

Introduction 7
    A Critical Examination 10
    Placebo 13

Sigmund Freud 15
  Totem and Taboo 17
  The Future of an Illusion 39
  Civilization and Its Discontents 49
  Moses and Monotheism 57
  The Stubborn Mind 71
    The Secret Committee 72

Freudians 79
  Karl Abraham 80
    Dreams and Myths 80
  Otto Rank 90
    The Birth of the Hero 90
    The Interpretation of Dreams 98
    The Trauma of Birth 104
    The Double 112
  Franz Riklin 116
    Sex in Fairy Tales 116
  Ernest Jones 121
    Spilling Salt 121
    A Dove in the Ear 124
    Effeminate God 127
  Oskar Pfister 130
    Psychoanalysis for Missionaries 131
    The Illusion of a Future of an Illusion 135
    Christianity as a Cure of Fear 140
  Theodor Reik 147
    Psychoanalytic Studies of Ritual 147
    Couvade 150

　　　　Oedipal Puberty Rites 156
　　Géza Róheim 163
　　　　Primitive Man and Environment 163
　　　　The Eternal Ones of the Dream 166
　　　　Always Oedipus 169
　　Helene Deutsch 172
　　　　Dionysus Saving his Mother 173
　　　　Apollo Killing Mothers 175
　　Erich Fromm 179
　　　　The Dogma of Christ 179
　　　　Escape from Freedom 190
　　　　Psychoanalysis and Religion 197
　　　　The Forgotten Language 206
　　　　You Shall Be as Gods 215
　　　　Shifting Perspectives 220

Literature 225
　　Web Sources 232

Introduction

The psychoanalytical perspective on mythology was unavoidable. When the study of myths and religions from all over the world intensified during the 19th century, patterns in them were extracted and compared, and theories on what they revealed about common human conditions were proposed. Myths were increasingly seen as expressions of needs of the human psyche.

The beliefs expressed in myths, as well as in rites, gradually ceased to be dismissed as merely heathen misconceptions as opposed to the sacred truth of the Christian doctrine. Instead, they became respected fields of study of the human nature, inspired by the quickly growing mass of documented myths and increasing knowledge about religious traditions among distant and obscure cultures.

By the end of the 19th century, the literature on the subject was immense, and mostly pointing to psychological explanations to the structure and content of myths, as well as for the birth of religions and their spiritual meaning.

To name a few:

English anthropologist Edward Burnett Tylor's *Primitive Culture: Researches into the Development of Mythology, Philosophy, Religion, Language, Art, and Custom* was published in 1871 and made a lasting impression. A few years earlier, in 1865, he had written *Researches into the Early History of Mankind* on the same theme.

The German philologist and orientalist Max Müller, who is regarded as the initiator of comparative religion, became Oxford's first professor of comparative theology in 1868. He edited *Sacred Books of the East*, published in 50 volumes from the years 1879 to 1910.

Scottish anthropologist James George Frazer's *The Golden Bough*, presenting a vast material on myth, lore, and ritual around the world, was originally published in 1890, as a two-volumes work. In the following decades it expanded considerably, reaching twelve volumes in its third edition, published between 1906 and 1915.

The Scottish author Andrew Lang's *Myth, Ritual, and Religion* in two volumes preceded Frazer by just a few years, getting published in 1887. There were also journals of anthropology published since the mid-1800's, frequently containing documentations of myths and rituals in nonliterate societies.

This rapid growth of interest in the traditions of other cultures was taking place simultaneously with the establishment of the science of psychology, and they influenced one another continuously. Anthropologists used psychological concepts to analyze and explain beliefs and religious practices of societies they studied, and psychologists searched anthropological material for support of their theories about the mentality of man. This is still the case.

The two persons most influential in the emergence of psychological treatments of myth were Sigmund Freud and Carl Gustav Jung, the latter to a much wider extent than the former. Since both were connected to the psychoanalytical movement — Freud as its founder and Jung as his most prominent disciple until they parted ways — and their perspectives on man and myth involved unconscious parts of the psyche supposed to play much more of a role than mere emotions and instinctive stimuli, it is possible to label their theories on myth psychoanalytical.

It can certainly be said about Freud's followers, who stuck with the term and what it contained. Jung was to change his name for the discipline to *analytical psychology*, which is not that different.

The term *depth psychology* is often used in this framework, but that would imply the existence of a shallow counterpart, which can be questioned, and it also suggests a vertical grading of the components of the psyche that is not necessarily shared by other psychologists.

By psychoanalytical perspectives on myths, I here refer to the theories of Freud, Jung, and their followers. For the 20th century, these two groups of theorists are so clearly defined that they can be treated as such without doing their individual thoughts any significant injustice. Freudians have treated myth and religion from the paradigm given by Freud, and Jungians have done the same from that of Jung.

For the future, though, both groups are sure to lose some of their homogeneity, since both Freudian and Jungian ideas about myth and religion are increasingly questioned and altered in differing directions, where they are not altogether abandoned. The latter seems to be more the case for Freud's ideas than for those of Jung. Freud has not stood the test of time to the extent that his former disciple has — especially in regard to theories about mythology, its psychological roots, and how it should be interpreted.

While Freud's psychology as a whole had a considerably wider reputation and respect than Jung's — and to some extent still does, although questioned on many central points — his take on myths in particular did not fare so well. There, Jung's influence grew to overshadow Freud all but completely, not that it has managed to find any consensus among either psychologists or mythologists.

This book deals exclusively with Sigmund Freud and his followers. A book about Jung and the Jungians is in the works. Initially, the project was intended to be one book, but it was getting rather voluminous. Also, the Freudian and Jungian theories differ so distinctly, there is little meaning in combining them in one text.

The Freudian perspective can be described as one of mythology stemming from personal urges that may be shared by all, but are strictly internal and based on each individual's instinctual emotions. Jungian theories, on the other hand, involve social causes and a symbolism formed and upheld by the human species, more or less independently of individual minds. Where Freudians see a pattern of instincts, Jungians point to imagination nurtured by cultural heritage. One focuses on strictly internal factors, and the other emphasizes external influence.

Although these two perspectives sometimes lead to similar conclusions regarding the causes and effects of myth and religion, they display fundamentally different views on the human psyche. So, they may just as well be treated separately, in order to explore each approach adequately.

In examining the Freudian theories about myth and religion, I have turned to their own writing on the subject, just about exclusively. Neither contemporary nor later commentators on their views are treated more than occasionally in passing, since their own words speak well for themselves and are enough material for an examination of them.

This book is about their theories on mythology, and not aiming at presenting other aspects of their psychology. It is also the reason for some significant Freudians being excluded for not treating the subject at hand in any substantial way, if at all. Only those who in their writing showed an interest in myth and religion are included. I may not have caught all of them, nor all of their writing on the subject, but I am confident that most of them are treated, as well as their most notable texts.

A Critical Examination

As is certainly evident in this book, my examination of the Freudians who theorized about the psychological causes behind mythology and religion is quite critical. I trust that it is also evident why. Anything else would be a betrayal of the book's objective. A serious investigation of this subject unavoidably leads to criticism, since there is such a discrepancy between Freudian claims and their arguments for them. So much is stated and so little is proven.

It is blatantly obvious already with what Sigmund Freud had to say about the emergence of religion and its constant fuel

— the Oedipus complex, which he regarded as the root to just about all expressions of the male psyche, and he would not even admit to the existence of something similar in the female mind.

The theory is, especially but not only when applied to religion, as preposterous as Freud's insistence on it is obstinate. He stuck with it until his death, refusing even to consider a nuanced view or alternative hypotheses. What he claimed to be a verified scientific theory was really a doctrine not to be questioned. A decree.

His followers were anxious to comply and did so with a reverence akin to that given high priests in religious congregations. This fidelity was clearly demonstrated by the formation and activities of the so-called Secret Committee, described in the last chapter of the text about Freud. That kind of loyalty is not unheard of in many kinds of subcultures, but it is gravely detrimental to scientific research.

The Freudians were more obsessed with defending Freud's dogma than trying to expand the understanding of the human psyche. This explains the high degree of conformity in their theories about mythology and religion. Those who followed other lines of thought were condemned and expelled.

The texts by the loyal ones can often be described as almost playful applications of Freud's paradigm on this or that myth or religious phenomenon, but they lack any questioning of the paradigm and they whisk away any anomaly they may come across. They are so happy with their tool, if not to say toy, by which they believe to make revelations about the mysteries of the human mind and its most intriguing manifestations. It is often strikingly naïve.

One must wonder how it was possible for so many pondering minds to get so lost. To a significant extent it can be explained by the cultish characteristics of the Freudian society, energetically promoted by its founder and master. Psychology, their field of expertise, was no vaccine against it. Instead, it may have dimmed their perception, thinking it could not happen to them because of their training. The ones who are the likeliest to be fooled are those who think they can't be.

But if that were the only reason, it would sooner or later be revealed and the participants would reconsider, with cheeks blushing from shame. What made this situation possible and consolidated it was the vague nature of the science in which they worked. Psychology was still very much limited to speculation and little was proven by hard empirical facts, during the first few decades of psychoanalysis.

Freud was convinced that the approach he pioneered was rooted in objective science, and he insisted in the beginning that only persons with a medical education could be entrusted with conducting psychoanalytical treatment. But there were — and to a large extent still are — substantial differences between science of the body and of the mind. The former can be systematically tested and the results are observable, usually measurable and often unquestionable, whereas the latter has difficulties with all of that.

Systematic testing of a psychological hypothesis is an intricate matter already because it is very difficult to repeat the test with a similar setting, which is necessary in an empirical process. Even if the hypothesis is defined with precision and clear delimitation, which is particularly problematic in psychology, repeated testing is not sure to isolate the item to be studied from other known or unknown variables. If the hypothesis is vague, the task is practically impossible.

The human mind is just too much of a maze to be trapped in repeated clinical experiments, without lots of circumstances bound to deviate from one test to the next. And people are far too different, in ways impossible to predict, for their results to be confidently compared even if the tests are deemed identical — in itself something very hard to assess.

In addition, the psyche is not enough understood and its processes not sufficiently mapped, for test results to be adequately observable and measurable in an empirically trustworthy manner. There are too many unknowns in the equation.

The simple cause and effect of, say, what the lack of one vitamin does to the body or how a broken bone is healed, is objectively observable. But that is rare to find in psychology. In the mind, everything is subjective. That gives room for speculations, but few affirmed conclusions.

What modern psychology often relies on to make conclusions are statistical correlations: more people than pure chance would have it react in a certain way to something. It is a precarious path of inquiry, and its application is limited to very simplified assumptions. Still, it is used a lot by psychologists, mainly because they have few other tools by which to experiment and get tangible results.

The psychoanalysts discussed in this book used a method to reach their conclusions, which was similar to the statistical one, but with alarming shortcomings. They referred to their experiences with patients treated by psychoanalysis, and used that as evidence of their theories. But those numbers were far too few to make any statistical evaluation, and they did not bother to present any figures. Instead, they regarded their thesis as true because they had patients whose behavior confirmed it. They often settled for just one case to prove their point, no matter how far-fetched or intricate it was.

As a method in empirical science, it has little value. It lacks any more weight than saying, "I once knew someone who was like that."

Placebo

There is another shortcoming in the psychoanalytical practice of using patients to prove a point, and it strikes at the core of psychoanalysis as a whole: How to ensure that a successful treatment is not the result of a psychological equivalent to placebo?

When a new medical drug is tested, a primary one to pass is if its effect surpasses that of placebo, the sugar pill substitution of the real medicine. Many do not. Placebo is a strong force, which is yet an example of the mysterious complexity of the human being, needed to be explained before anything certain can be said about the human psyche.

In psychoanalysis, there is an elaborate therapeutic setting, where the patient is guided towards what is to be expected and how to reach it. When that moment comes, patient and therapist rejoice and mutually regard the problem as solved. That is an ideal placebo situation — the process presented as a cure, led by the expert, and demanding the patient's trusting engagement. They cooperate in making it work, whether it would or not.

Reading a number of examples of psychoanalytical cures, I suspect that most or all of them could be explained by the placebo effect. I have not come across any psychoanalytical effort to check against this, and for a good reason — if it works on something as complicated as the human mind, why not leave it be?

What still needs to be considered is if the cure accomplished by psychoanalysis is a lasting one. I have not seen an eagerness within that profession to examine this aspect. A sudden revelation can be a great momentary relief, but if it was in error the problem is likely to return, given time.

So many of the psychoanalytical solutions give the impression of magic potions. Once the revelation is reached, everything is dandy. I find that hard to believe, and certainly not without some kind of evidence other than the psychoanalyst's assurance of it.

Of course, that particular topic goes beyond the scope of this book, which is not aimed at examining the theories and practices of psychoanalysis in their entirety. I am not even concerned with its possible benefits or damages in healthcare. But since psychoanalytical theories about myth and religion claim support through therapeutic experience, I would be negligent not to bring it up. This is one more indicator that those statements remain to be proven.

Sigmund Freud

Sigmund Freud was born in Moravia in 1856, but his family moved to Vienna only a few years later. In 1881 he graduated as an MD and worked in the Vienna General Hospital for a few years, also researching the clinical uses of cocaine. In 1885-86 he studied in Paris under Jean-Martin Charcot, a French neurologist who made pioneering research into hysteria.

The same year Freud returned from Paris, he started his own practice, where he treated nervous diseases and focused increasingly on psychology. In 1902 he was appointed professor extraordinaire of neurology at the University of Vienna, a position he held until he left for England in 1938, to escape Nazism.

In 1896, the same year his father died, Freud used the term *psychoanalysis* for the first time in a printed text. It was in an article about neurosis in a French magazine on neurology.[1] By the very end of the century, in November 1899, *Die Traumdeutung* (*The Interpretation of Dreams*) was published, but scarcely noticed for the first few years. An English translation was released in 1913.

In 1906 he befriended and started to cooperate with Carl G. Jung from Switzerland. Neither the friendship nor the cooperation would last, once their views on psychology started to differ.

There are three books in which Freud treated the subjects of myth and religion at depth. *Totem and Taboo* in 1913 presented theories that contradicted Jung's emerging models of

---

[1] Sigmund Freud, "L'Hérédité et l'étiologie des névroses" ("Heredity and the Aetiology of the Neuroses"), *Revue neurologique*, volume 4 (6), Paris, 1896, pp. 161-169.

explanation. In 1927 Freud published the essay *The Future of an Illusion*, where he discussed the origin of religion and clearly confessed to his own atheism. *Moses and Monotheism*, in which he persisted with the ideas presented in the previous texts, was published in 1939, the same year Freud died.

His book from 1930, *Civilization and Its Discontents*, is also discussed here although its topic is not mythology but the conflict between individual urges and social norms. Still, it treats religion, its emergence, and effects, which is why it should not be passed by.

Totem and Taboo

Freud's first text with a thorough examination of myth and religion using the tools of his own science is *Totem and Taboo* from 1913. The German subtitle translates to *Resemblances Between the Mental Lives of Savages and Neurotics*. Originally, it was published as four articles in his magazine *Imago* 1912-13. The first translation into English, by the psychiatrist Abraham Arden Brill who had also translated *The Interpretation of Dreams*, was published in 1918.

In the book, Freud refers to the pioneering psychologist Wilhelm Wundt (1832-1920) and Carl G. Jung as the first stimulus for his work on the subject.[2] In Jung's case he specifies the text *Transformations and Symbols of the Libido*, published in 1912.[3] However, Freud points out that his method "contrasts" both these sources. Wundt neglected to use analytic psychology, and Jung strove to "settle problems of individual psychology by referring to material of racial psychology."

Racial perspectives on psychology as well as on biology were, sadly, widely applied and respected in the scientific community of those days. So was the concept of the savage, which described people in hunter-gatherer societies and other cultures outside of modern industrial civilization as primitive remnants of earlier stages of human evolution.

Already the title *Totem and Taboo* indicates that this text relates to ritual more than to myth, searching for psychological explanations to certain traditions found in what Freud calls primitive society, as well as to some extent in his contemporary world. He compares taboo beliefs to neurosis, seeing both similarities and differences but expressing his belief in common psychological roots for them.

---

[2] Sigmund Freud, *Totem and Taboo*, transl. A. A. Brill, New York 1918, p. iii.

[3] The English title, published in 1916, was *Psychology of the Unconscious*.

He also boldly claims to explain the origin of religion, ethics, society, and art. That's just about all of mankind's major endeavors.

Skeptical Reception

His text was met with some skepsis — and still is, to say the least. Already in a 1914 review of the book, Carl Furtmüller, a former member of the Vienna Psychoanalytic Society, complained that Freud ignored critics, misused Darwin, and claimed the Oedipus complex to be the original sin of the human race. To Furtmüller, the book contained "the free play of fantasy."[4]

The cultural anthropologist Alfred Louis Kroeber reviewed the book in 1920 with equally harsh words. Although agreeing that psychology had an important place in ethnology, he dismissed Freud's conclusion that the beginnings of religion, ethics, society, and art meet in the Oedipus complex.[5] He dismissed or questioned eleven of Freud's arguments and called his reasoning insidious.

To Kroeber, Freud's book "substitutes a plan of multiplying into one another, as it were, fractional certainties — that is, more or less remote possibilities — without recognition that the multiplicity of factors must successively decrease the probability of their product."

His judgment was firm: "Freud cannot be charged with more than a propagandist's zeal and perhaps haste of composition."[6]

---

[4] Sigmund Freud & Otto Rank: *The Letters of Sigmund Freud and Otto Rank: Inside Psychoanalysis*, edited by E. James Lieberman and Robert Kramer, Baltimore 2012, pp. 37f.

[5] A. L. Kroeber, "Totem and Taboo: An Ethnologic Psychoanalysis," *American Anthropologist* vol. 22, 1920, p. 48.

[6] Ibid., pp. 51-53.

An Original Patricide

Freud had his own radical explanation to the birth of religion, which has mostly met with rejection close to ridicule from historians of religion. Still, he remained convinced of his theory, which he also declared in *Moses and Monotheism*, published the same year he died.

To his credit, he was already at the outset modest about the power of proof in his material. The fourth chapter of *Totem and Taboo*, where he presents his theory on the origin of religions, starts with the following obvious reservation, which passed unnoticed by some of his critics:

> *The reader need not fear that psychoanalysis, which first revealed the regular over-determination of psychic acts and formations, will be tempted to derive anything so complicated as religion from a single source.*[7]

On the other hand, later on in that long chapter, he claims:

> *I want to state the conclusion that the beginnings of religion, ethics, society, and art meet in the Oedipus complex. This is in entire accord with the findings of psychoanalysis, namely, that the nucleus of all neuroses as far as our present knowledge of them goes is the Oedipus complex.*[8]

Freud based his theory mainly on the psychoanalytical thesis of the Oedipus complex, and on totemism — to the point that he called this chapter of the book "The Infantile Recurrence of Totemism."

The term totemism was introduced in 1791 by John Long, who wrote about his experiences with Canadian natives.[9] At

---

[7] Freud, *Totem and Taboo*, p. 165.

[8] Ibid., p. 258.

[9] John Long, *Voyages and Travels of an Indian Interpreter and Trader*, London 1791, p. 87. He spelled it *totamism*.

the end of the 19th and beginning of the 20th century, there was a wide-spread fascination among anthropologists about totemism.

The phenomenon that a family or a clan had a ritualized symbolic relation to a specific animal species, with which they claimed to be linked or even related, was known beforehand. But it received increased attention through the Scottish researcher John Ferguson McLennan, who in 1869 presented the idea that totemism might lie behind a number of customs, where totemism itself had disappeared.[10]

What attracted Freud's interest was first and foremost:

Almost everywhere the totem prevails there also exists the law that the members of the same totem are not allowed to enter into sexual relations with each other; that is, that they cannot marry each other. This represents the exogamy which is associated with the totem.[11]

One would think that the rule against sexual intercourse within the clan was intended as a protection against incest and inbreeding, but to this Freud objects that he doubts such civilized behavior among the "primitive" people. He also claims, without presenting support for it, that the damaging effects of inbreeding are not ascertained. He strongly rejects the possibility of such awareness among the primitives of the past:

It sounds almost ridiculous to attribute hygienic and eugenic motives such as have hardly yet found consideration in our culture, to these children of the race who lived without thought of the morrow.[12]

---

[10] Andrew Lang, *Myth, Ritual & Religion*, volume I, London 1887, p. 59. Also in Freud, *Totem and Taboo*, p. 5 (footnote).

[11] Freud, *Totem and Taboo*, pp. 5f.

[12] Ibid., pp. 205f.

In a footnote to this statement, he takes support in Charles Darwin, quoting him about savages: "They are not likely to reflect on distant evils to their progeny." It is from the second edition of Darwin's *The Variation of Animals and Plant under Domestication*, but that wording is missing from the first edition. Darwin dismissed some contemporary theories about the reasons for prohibitions against marriages between kin:

> *But I cannot accept these views, seeing that incest is held in abhorrence by savages such as those of Australia and South America, who have no property to bequeath, or fine moral feelings to confuse, and who are not likely to reflect on distant evils to their progeny.*[13]

So, Freud shared with Darwin the conviction that societies seemingly simpler than their own were populated by simple minds, unable to observe what the consequences of inbreeding could be. They gave no sign of putting that thesis to the test.

In *Totem and Taboo*, Freud connects totemism's sexual restrictions to the Oedipus complex. He sees the totem as an image of a forefather, who had expelled his sons from the "horde" he ruled, to prevent them from having intercourse with the women of the horde. The sons would not have that: "One day the expelled brothers joined forces, slew and ate the father, and thus put an end to the father horde."[14]

As additional indication of this, Freud mentions the ritual meals documented in totemism, where the totem animal might get served. In a footnote to this passage, he refers to known similar behavior among some flock animals, also he claims support from Charles Darwin and from the anthropologist James Jasper Atkinson.

---

[13] Charles Darwin, *The Variation of Animals and Plant under Domestication*, vol. 2, 2nd edition, London 1875, p. 103. The 1st edition was published in 1868.

[14] Freud, *Totem and Taboo*, p. 234.

The latter's 1903 book *Primal Law* is quoted:

A youthful band of brothers living together in forced celibacy, or at most in polyandrous relation with some single female captive. A horde as yet weak in their impubescence they are, but they would, when strength was gained with time, inevitably wrench by combined attacks renewed again and again, both wife and life from the paternal tyrant.[15]

Freud refers to Charles Darwin about his theories on the primal social state of man:

From the habits of the higher apes Darwin concluded that man, too, lived originally in small hordes in which the jealousy of the oldest and strongest male prevented sexual promiscuity.[16]

Freud definitely thinks that the patricide had taken place in a distant past, but admits that he may have comprised the development of events, and ends an extensive footnote:

It would be just as meaningless to strive for exactness in this material as it would be unfair to demand certainty here.[17]

Freud moves on to claim that the guilt of the sons, and a wish for some kind of reconciliation, made them start to worship their dead father like a god, in the form of a totem, and to

---

[15] Quoted from James Jasper Atkinson, *Primal Law*, published in 1903 in a volume also containing Andrew Lang, *Social Origins*, which dealt with totemism, too. Andrew Lang & James Jasper Atkinson, *Social Origins & Primal Law*, London 1903, pp. 220f.

[16] Freud, *Totem and Taboo*, p. 207.

[17] Ibid., p. 235.

restrain their sexual habits by exogamy, seeking their mates outside the herd. This was also necessary for them in order to keep their group loyalty and avoid competing to repeat the behavior of their father:

> *Thus there was nothing left for the brothers, if they wanted to live together, but to erect the incest prohibition — perhaps after many difficult experiences — through which they all equally renounced the women whom they desired, and on account of whom they had removed the father in the first place.* [18]

He goes on to suggest that the bond between these men was one formed during their banishment, probably deepened by homosexual tendencies while they were deprived of female companions. In the guilt-triggered glorification of the father, Freud sees the insoluble tension that nourishes religion:

> *All later religions prove to be attempts to solve the same problem, varying only in accordance with the stage of culture in which they are attempted and according to the paths which they take; they are all, however, reactions aiming at the same great event with which culture began and which ever since has not let mankind come to rest.*[19]

Somewhat triumphantly, Freud ends his book by stating: "In the beginning was the deed."[20]

A Male World
Freud's theory describes a very male world, indeed. The women are but objects of desire, completely passive and insignificant in any other way. If he at all admits them to wrestle

[18] Ibid., p. 237.
[19] Ibid., p. 239.
[20] Ibid., p. 265.

with their own problems of the soul — and there is no mention of it in *Totem and Taboo* — the women have no active role at all in the formation of religion. One wonders why they would care to participate in the worship of that father figure.

Freud was far from alone neglecting female influence in society, at the time he wrote his book as well as long before and after it. Indeed, society at his time was ruled almost exclusively by men. But there were exceptions.

He wrote his text little more than a decade after the death of Queen Victoria in 1901. She was a very prominent figure all over the world during her long reign. That was when Great Britain was by far the most powerful of countries, its rule reaching so far that the sun was rightly said never to set on the empire.

Women had made their marks in other fields as well. The Nobel Prize shows evidence of it. Marie Curie got it in physics 1903 and then again in chemistry 1911. Selma Lagerlöf got it in literature 1909, and she was far from the only female writer read and admired by millions. Bertha von Suttner was awarded the Nobel Peace Prize in 1905. The list of prominent women at the time Freud wrote his book can be made quite long, but suffice to say that he cannot have been unaware of female influence in society, also in fields where men dominated overwhelmingly.

Even more alarming in his case is that he studied the human psyche and its manifestations. How to do that while excluding the influence of half of humankind?

If men were driven in their actions by competing over the women, how could the behavior of the objects of their desire be neglectable? There could be no Oedipus complex without women.

It is hard to comprehend how Freud could spend so much of his intellectual effort on the theory of the Oedipus complex without considering — or even discussing — the importance of the woman's role in this drama.

Carl G. Jung did so, already in 1912. He introduced the

female counterpart to the Oedipus complex, calling it the Electra complex after the princess in Greek mythology, who plotted to have her mother killed:

> *In the case of the son, the conflict develops in a more masculine and therefore more typical form, whilst in the daughter, the typical affection for the father develops, with a correspondingly jealous attitude toward the mother. We call this complex, the Electra-complex.*[21]

But Freud rejected the term. In a footnote to a 1920 essay on female homosexuality he states: "I do not see any progress or advantage in the introduction of the term 'Electra-complex,' and do not advocate its use."[22] He strongly denied the possibility of a female counterpart to the Oedipus complex. In his essay *Female Sexuality* from 1931 he writes:

> *We have the impression that what we have said about that complex applies in all strictness only to male children, and that we are right in rejecting the term "Electra complex" which seeks to insist that the situation of the two sexes is analogous. It is only in male children that there occurs the fateful simultaneous conjunction of love for the one parent and hatred of the other as rival.*[23]

The firmness of Freud's prejudiced statement is equaled by the folly of its claim. In this particular context, what stands out is the crack it makes in his theory. The greater he proposes the impact of the Oedipus complex to be on society and its in-

---

[21] Carl G. Jung, *The Theory of Psychoanalysis*, New York 1915, p. 69. The German original, *Versuch einer Darstellung der psychoanalytischen*, was published in 1913.

[22] Sigmund Freud, *Sexuality and the Psychology of Love*, New York 1963, p. 141.

[23] Ibid., pp. 197f.

habitants, the bigger the need gets to explain the absence of half of them in his model.

The genders interact. Women act upon what men do, and vice versa. So did Jocasta in the Sophocles drama, when finding out that her spouse Oedipus was also her son. And in *Lysistrata*, the Aristophanes comedy from the same period, the women play the men as if they were puppies. What would not the women do if a patriarch expelled their brothers, sons, and lovers? One thing is for sure — they would not worship him, dead or alive.

History shows no sign of religion being an exclusively male undertaking. Worship has been as devout from both sexes. Therefore, it must have other sources than one that applies only to men.

Freud needed to make the women passive bystanders in order for his theory to compute. Otherwise, it would fail to explain that through the millennia, religion has attracted both sexes. He made religion an exclusively male thing.

Certainly, men have been in firm control of the higher offices of religion, especially in the three monotheisms. Paul expressed it in his first letter to the Corinthians:

> *Let your women keep silence in the churches: for it is not permitted unto them to speak; but they are commanded to be under obedience as also saith the law. And if they will learn any thing, let them ask their husbands at home: for it is a shame for women to speak in the church.*[24]

Catholicism continues to use it as an excuse to refuse female priests. But in Protestantism, the exceptions are countless and the attitude another — as of lately. But never have women been forbidden to worship and partake in the rituals and celebrations of those religions.

Both sexes have always been expected to be faithful to

---

[24] 1 Corinthians 14:34-35, *King James Bible*.

their god. That god may be described as male, but he is still the god of both men and women.

The only way Freud's theory of the origin of religion could make sense, would be if women had been excluded from worship, and happily so. A purely male need for religion would hardly raise a need for it in women. That is definitely not what history has shown. Religion has proven to fill a need for men and women alike.

Irrelevant to Polytheism
Another striking omission in Freud's theory as presented in *Totem and Taboo* is that of polytheism. The sovereign primordial father god of the monotheisms is hard to find in polytheistic religions, which are most of them.

Strictly speaking, only three religions are monotheistic — and they are closely related: Judaism, Christianity, and Islam. The other ones are either clearly polytheistic or vague about gods as such.

Well, there is such a variety of religions and mythologies over the world and through the millennia, any simplified sorting of them is bound to have numerous exceptions. There are or have been other religions fitting the definition of monotheism just as well as the three Abrahamic ones. That can be said about Zoroastrianism, Sikhism, and Pharaoh Akhenaton's short-lived sun god worship mentioned by Freud in his book *Moses and Monotheism*.

Still, the monotheism Freud discusses, with a fatherly high-god who is the creator of the world and whose power is unmatched by any other, fits but few of the religions we know, compared to the vast number of polytheisms in the world now and in the past. Freud's model of an original patricide fails to explain polytheism, although for sure there are lots of patricides in their mythologies, even among the gods.

The oldest known example of this is from ancient Mesopotamian mythology, where the fresh water god Apsu, who is the mate of the salt water goddess Tiamat, is killed by his son

Ea. The story is told in the Babylonian text *Enuma Elish*, composed in the 2nd millennium BC, but the Sumerian origin of the myth may be one or even two thousand years older. In spite of the patricide, the Sumerian and Babylonian mythologies are exceedingly polytheistic.

A classical example from Greek mythology of the battle between father and son, also with quite a Freudian ingredient, is Cronus castrating and overthrowing his father Uranus. The sickle he used was given to him by his mother Gaia, who encouraged the deed. Cronus, in turn, was gutted by his son Zeus, who had good reason for it. Thereby he released other children of Cronus who had been devoured by him.

Still, Greek religion cannot by any means be called monotheistic in the sense of worshipping only an elevated father figure. The Greek pantheon had a sovereign in Zeus, but he was far from the only one worshipped. Nor was there any overwhelming male dominance of gods, either in number or in feats.

With or without patricide, the polytheistic religions — and there are lots of them — remain anomalies to Freud's paradigm. He had no explanation to their emergence. That should have told him he might have been wrong about the emergence of monotheism, as well.

Alternative Explanations
Another thing lacking in *Totem and Taboo* is the exploration of what possible alternative explanations to the emergence of religion there might be, whether or not only in monotheism. Without at least trying other possibilities, if only to dismiss them, Freud could not have had much trust in his own hypothesis.

Instead, Freud spent his text listing the examples and circumstances that might support his theory, at least not refute them. It is about as solid as picking a few black cats to prove that all cats are black. There are lots of cats. There are also lots of religions and lots of theories to explain their emergence.

Granted, at the time Freud wrote his book there were not as many theories about the origin of religion as there are now, but still they were not few. One of the oldest is that of the Greek statesman Critias, who was the uncle of Plato, living in the 5th century BC. His very blunt view on religion and its source was expressed in a satyr-play of his, *Sisyphus*, where the title role explains:

> *There was a time when the life of men was unordered, bestial and the slave of force, when there was no reward for the virtuous and no punishment for the wicked. Then, I think, men devised retributory laws, in order that Justice might be dictator and have arrogance as its slave, and if anyone sinned, he was punished. Then, when the laws forbade them to commit open crimes of violence, and they began to do them in secret, a wise and clever man invented fear (of the gods) for mortals, that there might be some means of frightening the wicked, even if they do anything or say or think it in secret. Hence, he introduced the Divine, saying that there is a God flourishing with immortal life, hearing and seeing with his mind, and thinking of everything and caring about these things, and having divine nature, who will hear everything said among mortals, and will be able to see all that is done.*[25]

I must say that I find the old Critias claim much more convincing, already at first glance, than that of Freud. In its simplicity it also passes the test of Ockham's razor smoothly, by not needing a much-specified series of events and equally specified human reactions to them.

But Critias's theory about the birth of religions was far from the only one around, at the time Freud wrote his book. A little more than a century after Critias, Euhemerus suggested that the myths were enhanced accounts of ancient history, and

---

[25] Freeman, Kathleen, *The Pre-Socratic Philosophers*, Oxford 1946, p. 157.

the gods were kings and heroes of old. His theory was later to be repeated by others, to the point that this kind of explanation was given his name: *euhemerism*.

In the Christian era, speculating about the origin of religion being anything else than God's creation of man was blasphemous and could very well lead to the capital punishment. But that changed in the 19th century, when religion started to be examined scientifically instead of just theologically. Not that such scrutiny was readily applied to Christianity, but as the emerging science of religion scanned all the other religions explored around the world, the inclusion of Christianity in the analysis was unavoidable and at length unstoppable.

Max Müller, a 19th century pioneer of the scientific study of religion, was careful to point out that his findings related to "heathen" religions and gods, when presenting his idea that they were the results of a disease of language. Words depicting ordinary natural phenomena turned by time into mythology, in which "heathen gods are nothing but poetical names, which were gradually allowed to assume a divine personality never contemplated by their original inventors."[26]

Müller's reasoning is not far from that of Euhemerus, but Müller transforms it to encompass all of nature, not just enhanced descriptions of prominent people of the past. Some of his examples are obvious, such as the planets being turned into deities. That is the case in many more mythologies than those of Ancient Greece and Rome.

The English anthropologist Edward B. Tylor, who is regarded as a major pioneer in the fields of cultural as well as social anthropology, made a lasting impression on the research of mythology with his work *Primitive Culture*, published in 1871. Tylor's main theory, on which he based his analysis of mythology as well as other cultural manifestations of what he called primitive society, is that of animism, the belief that there is life in many or all objects and phenomena.

---

[26] Max Müller, *Lectures on the Science of Language*, London 1861, p. 11.

This aspect dominates his text. Of the book's 19 chapters, seven are devoted to the theme of animism already in their titles. Still, it appears frequently in the other chapters, too. Tylor regarded animism to be the cause of mythology as a whole:

First and foremost among the causes which transfigure into myth the facts of daily experience, is the belief in the animation of all nature, rising at its highest pitch to personification.[27]

Thus, the gods as well as the other active characters of myths were born out of animism. Tylor saw it as an application of analogy — what seems like something must in some way be that something. What we use as poetic metaphor and such, had quite another significance in the distant past: "Analogies which are but fancy to us were to men of past ages reality."[28]

He compared it to the experience of the child, unable to make distinctions between reality and the impressions of it. He quoted from Victor Hugo's *Les Misérables* about Cosette and her doll, "imagine that something is someone."[29] Tylor likened the intellect of the human species in its early stage to that of children and childlike ideas, "in our childhood we dwelt at the very gates of the realm of myth."[30]

To Tylor, this childhood is something that civilized man of the Western world has left behind, and he was far from alone at that time to think so. It can be debated. A more interesting line of thought is that of childhood per se, in all times and all cultures, and what makes children so delighted to let their minds wander into the realm of myths. They don't seem to do so out of fear or angst, but with joy.

---

[27] Edward B. Tylor, *Primitive Culture: Researches into the Development of Mythology, Philosophy, Religion, Art, and Custom*, vol. 1, London 1871, p. 258.

[28] Ibid., p. 269.

[29] "Se figurer que quelque chose est quelqu'un." Ibid., p. 258.

[30] Ibid., p. 257.

Freud's explanation of the emergence and role of mythology lacks that ingredient of joy completely, although it is evident among adults as well. Mythology has always intrigued us and worship has more often than not been celebratory. This, too, puts Freud's theory into question.

Another pioneer of the scientific study of mythology was James G. Frazer, whose writing Freud refers to frequently in *Totem and Taboo*. Frazer's major contribution to the study of myth was his extensive work *The Golden Bough* from 1890, with much expanded editions following.

Frazer's basic theory was that primitive man long ago was trying magic, first and foremost in fertility cults, as a means to control aspects of life that were beyond hands-on control. This magic evolved into religion, which in turn much later evolved into science. So, he defined magic as a kind of pseudo-science. When it failed to provide sufficient results, people had to accept the power of fate, and magic was replaced by prayers and sacrifice.[31]

Yet, regarding the very origin of religious beliefs, Frazer later developed the firm conviction that it depended on the fear of the dead. He stated it very clearly in the preface to the abridged edition of *The Golden Bough*, published in 1922, "the fear of the human dead, which, on the whole, I believe to have been probably the most powerful force in the making of primitive religion."[32]

Later, he wrote a book on this subject, *The Fear of the Dead in Primitive Religion*, where he repeated his credo, "there can be little doubt that the fear of the dead has been a prime source of primitive religion."[33] This book was his last major work.

---

[31] James G. Frazer, *The Golden Bough: A Study in Comparative Religion*, vol. 1, London 1890, p. 31.

[32] James G. Frazer, *The Golden Bough: A study of magic and religion*, abridged edition, New York 1922, p. vii.

[33] James G. Frazer, *The fear of the dead in primitive religion*, London 1933, p. v.

It should be noted that he was not talking about the fear of death, but living people's fear of those who had died. It would be so much easier to follow his chain of thought if he were to describe the significance of the fear of death — not the dead — in the cults, rituals, and mythologies of religions.

Frazer's theory about the fear of the dead would not have reached Freud when he wrote *Totem and Taboo*, but that about magic developing into religious worship most likely had. Frazer and other anthropologists writing about mythology were not exclusively examining the monotheisms. Therefore, they were able to see other patterns in the emergence of religions and their rites than Freud allowed in his perspective.

The major difference between those anthropologists and Freud is that where the former speculated about religion diversifying and developing through time, much like the evolution discovered by Charles Darwin, Freud presented religion as something once born, for one reason, and that was it. Of course, this is only possible to claim at all if just looking at the Abrahamic monotheisms, which do have one common source.

Something Worth Pondering?
Although Freud's theory about the origin of religion being one and the same for all religions is its major weakness, it remains a perspective worth investigating.

Beliefs in supernatural powers, executed by more or less anthropomorphic beings whose existence elude scrutiny, are found all through known history and in any society. These traditions certainly differ so much that terms like religion and gods fail to describe them all adequately, but they do share some common denominators. Freud's examination was an effort to describe what they may have in common at their roots. He failed to prove that his explanation was the right one, but he pointed out the value of the search.

For example, human fear of the unknown is evident in every mythology I have come across. Death is not the least of those fears. Maybe a theory based on human anguish about death would further our understanding of how religions appeared. Death is something we know that none of us can escape, and yet we really know nothing about where that passage might or might not lead. All mythologies treat death extensively and no society in recorded history is completely free of rites related to its occurrence.

Christianity and Islam have soothing assurances about an afterlife — and, of course, nightmarish alternatives for the wicked. That can be found in polytheism as well. But contrary to the idea of blissful existence in the beyond, several of the ancient mythologies depict a most gruesome afterlife, which could in no way be comforting for the believer. Often the realm of the dead is a netherworld, from which there is no escape and in which there is no solace.

The *Epic of Gilgamesh* is the oldest substantial work of literature remaining. Its most ancient version is from the 18th century BC, but the text is probably a few hundred years older than that. Gilgamesh's companion Enkidu, who is ridden by fear of imminent death, visits the netherworld in a dream. It is not a pleasant sight.

> *He bound my arms like the wings of a bird,*
> *to lead me captive to the house of darkness, seat of Irkalla:*
> *to the house which none who enters ever leaves,*
> *on the path that allows no journey back,*
> *to the house whose residents are deprived of light,*
> *where soil is their sustenance and clay their food,*
> *where they are clad like birds in coats of feathers,*
> *and see no light, but dwell in darkness.*[34]

The Egyptian *Book of the Dead* is a collection of texts by priests over a long period, where the oldest parts are from the 3rd millennium BC. It is a manual of sorts for how to manage in the realm of the dead by methods mainly of magical spells

---

[34] *The Epic of Gilgamesh*, transl. Andrew George, London 1999, p. 61.

and offerings. It is not an easy matter, and great perils are at stake. What is needed to navigate somewhat safely through that domain is hardly accessible to others than the most fortunate and wealthy — initially none other than the pharaoh.

Success in this complicated quest would lead to a formidable eternal life as someone akin to the gods. According to some texts, probably of later date, the final test is a weighing of the heart ritual, measuring sinfulness. But against this, too, there are magic spells guaranteeing a good outcome, whatever deeds one has committed in life.

Although there are terrible monsters to overcome along the way, as well as many precautions absolutely necessary in order to proceed, there is no explicit mention of the outcome for failure — except being killed by one of those monsters. What is implied is how crucial it is to avoid failure. Without the tools of the book, the afterlife has no hope. So, failure is out of the question, which is probably why it is not described in any detail. E. A. Wallis Budge, translator of the texts, writes:

> *Of the condition of those who failed to secure a life of beatitude with the gods in the Sekhet-Aaru of the Tuat, the pyramid texts say nothing, and it seems as if the doctrine of punishment of the wicked and of the judgment which took place after death is a development characteristic of a later period.*[35]

Still, the mythology of the book serves as a setting in which safe travel to a splendid afterlife is possible. In this way, it brings hope of something good waiting on the other side of death. A belief of that kind must be comforting — at least to the pharaoh.

Some other mythologies are much more generous. There is the Norse belief in the afterlife Valhalla, where the Vikings

---

[35] E. A. Wallis Budge, *The Book of the Dead: The Papyrus of Ani*, first edition 1895, New York 1967, p. cvi.

can forever do battle each day and feast each night — as long as they have died in battle. That would be heaven to a Viking.

> *Every morning, when they have dressed themselves, they take their weapons and go out into the court and fight and slay each other. That is their play. Toward breakfast-time they ride home to Valhal and sit down to drink.*[36]

Even Buddhism, with its principle of reincarnation, soothes the mind of man worrying about death. It explains what will happen, and even though the ultimate ideal is ceasing to exist, its believers will have the benefit of knowing what is ahead. They can also take comfort in being reborn before that ultimate step.

The Indian religions were not the only ones to contain the idea of reincarnation. Several of the Greek philosophers had a similar idea, calling it *metempsychosis*, starting with Pherecydes of Syros in the 6th century BC. Pythagoras, said to be his pupil, developed this idea more. Diogenes Laertius even has him inventing it:

> *He was the first, they say, to declare that the soul, bound now in this creature, now in that, thus goes on a round ordained of necessity.*[37]

Pythagoras's own metempsychosis was a trick played on the gods to achieve a kind of immortality:

> *This is what Heraclides of Pontus tells us he used to say about himself: that he had once been Aethalides and was*

---

[36] *The Younger Edda*, transl. Rasmus B. Anderson, Chicago 1880, p. 107. The Eddas are collections of Norse mythology and legends written down by Snorri Sturluson in the 13th century.

[37] Diogenes Laertius, *Lives of Eminent Philosophers*, vol. 2, transl. R. D. Hicks, London 1925, p. 333.

accounted to be Hermes' son, and Hermes told him he might choose any gift he liked except immortality; so he asked to retain through life and through death a memory of his experiences. Hence in life he could recall everything, and when he died he still kept the same memories.[38]

By this device Pythagoras protected what is the essence of immortality — the preservation of one's memories. There is no point to an afterlife that lacks recollection of previous experiences. Strictly speaking, without remembering the former life it is no afterlife at all — just another life.

Plato, too, expressed belief in metempsychosis. It is through his writing that the subject reached attention in the Western world. He regarded the soul as indestructible, wherefore it would wander on after the death of the body to occupy another body. Since souls are indestructible, there is also a fixed number of them:

But if it is so, you will observe that these souls must always be the same. For if none perishes they could not, I suppose, become fewer nor yet more numerous. For if any class of immortal things increased you are aware that its increase would come from the mortal and all things would end by becoming immortal.[39]

All those belief systems we call religions have in common that they do — one way or other — explain what happens when we die. Even if that is something far worse than what life offers, at least it is a kind of clarification. What can be more frightening than the complete unknown? This is what Shakespeare pointed out in the famous monologue in which Hamlet contemplates suicide:

---

[38] Ibid., p. 323.

[39] Plato, *Republic*, transl. Paul Shorey, volume 2, book X:611, London 1942, p. 479.

> *Who would fardels bear,*
> *to grunt and sweat under a weary life,*
> *but that the dread of something after death,*
> *the undiscover'd country from whose bourn*
> *no traveller returns, puzzles the will,*
> *and makes us rather bear those ills we have,*
> *than fly to others that we know not of.*[40]

And there is much more of the unknown explained by mythology. For example, myths tell how it all began and how it will end in the future, why seasons change, why day is followed by night, what wakes up the winds, what makes rain fall, and just about everything else incomprehensible to people of our distant past.

In particular, the unpredictable blows of fate were not only explained as the work of deities hidden from view, but there were methods of magic or worship by which to please those deities and gain a better fortune. Something could be done even about things that were totally incomprehensible.

In short, questions that arose in the wondering human mind could be answered by its own imagination.

There are, most definitely, common denominators to be found in the origins of the religions. But the patricide of Freud's theory is not one of them.

---

[40] William Shakespeare, "Hamlet, Prince of Denmark," act 3 scene 1, *The Complete Works of William Shakespeare*, London 1973, p. 862.

The Future of an Illusion

In 1927, 14 years after publishing *Totem and Taboo,* Freud wrote an essay on the subject of religion, its causes and function, in which he presented a broader view than just that of eternal remorse after a distant patricide.

In *The Future of an Illusion,* Freud confirms his theory of the Oedipus complex being at the root of religion, but he also recognizes causes and effects that have a wider scope, such as the human need to tackle fear of the unknown, discussed above. In particular, "the painful riddle of death, against which no medicine has yet been found, nor probably will be."[41]

Enemies of Civilization
Freud describes the human condition as one of suffering from the tension between nature and civilization.[42] It is against the uncertainties and difficulties of the former that the latter is a guard. Still, Freud states firmly, "every individual is virtually an enemy of civilization."[43]

This animosity towards the very thing that can improve life beyond what nature alone would allow, Freud explains as caused by the suppression of human urges and instincts. As for those urges, Freud's perception of human nature is not flattering: "Among these instinctual wishes are those of incest, cannibalism and lust for killing."[44] It is to appease people, in spite of this restraint, that religious ideas have taken their forms. According to Freud, the gods (now he speaks of a plural) have three major functions:

---

[41] Sigmund Freud, *The Future of an Illusion (Die Zukunft einer Illusion, 1927),* transl. James Strachey, New York 1961, p. 16.

[42] Freud uses the German word *Kultur,* which can be translated as both culture and civilization, depending on the context. Ibid., 4.

[43] Ibid., p. 6.

[44] Ibid., p. 10.

> *The gods retain their threefold task: they must exorcize the terrors of nature, they must reconcile men to the cruelty of Fate, particularly as it is shown in death, and they must compensate them for the sufferings and privations which a civilized life in common has imposed on them.*[45]

Freud also describes a development of the roles of gods, as humans got to understand more of the world around them. Many phenomena of nature showed to be autonomous, in no need of continuous divine activity. So, the gods were focused on their third task, helping people deal with the frustration of conforming to civilization. This was mainly a question of morality, since it dealt not only with man's imperfections but also with those of civilization. The order imposed by civilization was on divine decree:

> *Everything that happens in this world is an expression of the intentions of an intelligence superior to ours, which in the end, though its ways and byways are difficult to follow, orders everything for the best — that is, to make it enjoyable for us.*[46]

Therefore, obedience towards such a deity would be the only way to have a life as pleasant as possible. At least, that was the idea. Freud shows little trust in it actually having worked out well:

> *It is doubtful whether men were in general happier at a time when religious doctrines held unrestricted sway; more moral they certainly were not.*[47]

---

[45] Ibid., p. 18.
[46] Ibid., p. 19.
[47] Ibid., p. 37.

Towards Science

The development of religion and then away from it, Freud compares to childhood needs and growing out of them. The comfort of religious beliefs belonged to primitive man of the distant past, like children need to have faith in being protected by their parents — especially, if not exclusively, by their father. At length, though, mankind needs to replace religion with science and leave those childhood beliefs behind.

He states that this is happening, at least in Europe and in "the higher strata of human society."[48] As for the rest of the people, he doesn't have very high hopes:

> *Probably a certain percentage of mankind (owing to a pathological disposition or an excess of instinctual strength) will always remain asocial; but if it were feasible merely to reduce the majority that is hostile towards civilization to-day into a minority, a great deal would have been accomplished — perhaps all that* can *be accomplished.*[49]

As an example of how it can still go wrong, he mentions the "monkey trial" at Dayton, Tennessee, in 1925. A science teacher was prosecuted for teaching that "man is descended from the lower animals."[50] Freud mentions nothing more about the case, in which the teacher John Thomas Scopes was fined $100. But in an appeal, the fine was removed since its size had been decided incorrectly in the previous court.[51]

Freud's essay is mainly an argument for society to leave the illusions of religion behind, and turn its trust to science. In spite of glitches like the "monkey trial" he does have hope for humanity growing out of this infancy:

---

[48] Ibid., p. 38.
[49] Ibid., p. 9.
[50] Ibid., p. 38.
[51] Scopes Trial, *Wikipedia*.

The voice of the intellect is a soft one, but it does not rest till it has gained a hearing. Finally, after a countless succession of rebuffs, it succeeds. This is one of the few points on which one may be optimistic about the future of mankind, but it is in itself a point of no small importance.[52]

He ends his essay with a reference to its title:

No, our science is no illusion. But an illusion it would be to suppose that what science cannot give us we can get elsewhere.[53]

What he hopes for is that the future of the religious illusion will be short. As for the origin of the deity to fulfill the above-mentioned comforts, Freud remains with his theory from *Totem and Taboo* of a primeval patricide:

Religion would thus be the universal obsessional neurosis of humanity; like the obsessional neurosis of children, it arose out of the Oedipus complex, out of the relation to the father.[54]

He would stick to his theory also in his last book, *Moses and Monotheism*, published the same year he died. He was nothing if not persistent.

Nature versus Civilization

Freud claimed that the conflict between nature and civilization was the reason for human discomfort and led to — among other things — the emergence of religion. But nature and civilization are not opposites.

Civilization is not an artifact born out of some brilliant or

---

[52] Freud, *The Future of an Illusion*, p. 53.

[53] Ibid., p. 56.

[54] Ibid., p. 43.

vicious mind of the past. It is not separate from nature, but has occurred within it, so to speak naturally. All humans, as far back as we can trace, have formed societies increasing in complexity over time — often in rigidity, as well. That is what our species does. It is in our nature.

Ours is far from the only species doing that. Look at the intricacies of how ants and bees are organized, how herds of buffalo move in unison, and great flocks of birds form patterns as they fly through the sky. Any animal species, where the individuals do not live in absolute solitude, is organized in more or less complex societies to which they adapt as a matter of instinct.

Civilization is part of nature. That does not mean we adapt to it without friction and frustration. Surely not. But very few of us would prefer to live outside it or see it totally ruined. Nothing would be more frustrating to us than to be excluded from it.

Even Freud's essay hints at it, when discussing why suppressed classes accept unfair treatment in a society where only few profit from it. He thinks it must be because the masses are "emotionally attracted to their masters" and "see in them their ideals." Without some such kind of explanation, "it would be impossible to understand how a number of civilizations have survived so long in spite of the justifiable hostility of large human masses."[55]

There may very well be other reasons for the suppressed masses accepting their situation, such as brute force in the hands of their oppressors. But it should also be taken into account that they are content, because they are themselves defenders and not enemies of civilization.

That is indeed what history shows us. Most members of any society are defenders of it, not enemies to it.

---

[55] Ibid., p. 13.

Incest, Cannibalism, and Killing
People are also defenders of the values and regulations their society professes. Few would indulge in incest, cannibalism and killing, nor would they approve of others doing so.

As for cannibalism, or with a fancier word *anthropophagy*, civilization in the meaning of a regulated society is not a perfect safeguard against it. Except for occasions of starvation in crisis situations and the rare examples of criminal cannibalism committed by individuals, the instances of cannibalism examined by anthropologists and historians indicate that it was at the time socially accepted behaviors within those groups. Cannibalism was not only accepted in those situations, but encouraged, if not demanded in ritualistic habits. Such civilizations promoted cannibalism instead of suppressing it.[56]

As for killing, it may be illegal for individuals in most civilizations, but it is done collectively in quantities widely surpassing any one individual's urge or ability. The capital punishment, wars, and even genocides, are all inventions of civilization. Our present society is still very far from putting a stop to it. Instead, we have become ever more efficient at it.

Freud wrote his essay in 1927, which was a period when Europe had gone through a war so terrible that a repetition was unthinkable. But just a few years later, that had changed. And still today, nations arm themselves for annihilation. Our species would be safer from itself if we were unable to form civilizations.

It can be argued that these terrible shortcomings of civilization may be due to its acceptance, sometimes even encouragement, of the worst sides of man. If our species is by nature brutal, we should not be surprised if our civilization is, as well. But if that is the case, Freud's theory offers no solution. It would instead mean that civilization is not immune to what he regarded as our dreadful nature. Instead of man being re-

---

[56] For anthropological studies of cannibalism, see Paula Brown & Donald F. Tuzin (ed.), *The Ethnography of Cannibalism*, Washington D.C. 1983.

formed by society, he would simply form it to his liking. So, we would do neither better nor worse without it. There is no guarantee that civilization will be civilized.

Incest is a somewhat different matter, since it does not necessarily mean brutalization by one person of another. It might also be consensual. Still, it is condemned in most societies and has been for very long. As mentioned earlier, Freud theorized about it in *Totem and Taboo*, where he claimed that the taboo of incest stems from the Oedipus complex.

But there are anomalies in civilization's attitude towards incest and inbreeding. It is a matter of how far to take it. Many societies tend to frown upon finding a mate outside of it, even outside one's own sub-group within that society. Those sub-groups can be quite narrow, involving age, ethnicity, class, and what-not. Aristocrats and royalties tend to restrict marriage and procreation to the few of their own stratum. Especially in the case of royalties, it can become quite close to inbreeding.

The whole idea of mating within one's own kind, particularly upheld by the ruling classes of many societies, is incestuous at its core. Still, it is regarded as very civilized, indeed.

So, it can just as easily be said that civilization increases the occurrences and severity of incest, cannibalism and killing, instead of preventing them. Still, we tend to cherish our civilization — though certainly not because of these tendencies. Freud is not alone in seeing the benefits of an orderly society. We can all see it. To the masses as well as to their rulers, civilization is a good thing, in spite of its in some cases ghastly shortcomings.

Solace Instead of Fear
Of course, our willing commitment to civilization does not necessarily disprove Freud's idea about civilization developing in such a way that man's frustration towards it made religion arise as a kind of remedy. But it puts in question his statement that this would be universal and unavoidable because of some fundamental conflict between nature and civilization.

Since the formation of civilizations is more natural for us than having none, as history has proven, this tendency alone cannot explain what appears in these civilizations. Each phenomenon must be examined for what it implies about any underlying mechanism, and that may very well differ from one society to another.

Freud's claim that the illusion of a divine origin to the rules of society was to increase human trust in them is not far from what Critias in Ancient Greece suggested, as mentioned previously: Gods were invented to scare people into obedience of the laws. But where Critias speaks of fear, Freud points to solace. Religion gave mankind the illusion of fate being governed by a higher wisdom, leading ultimately to something good and fair. People could put faith in their god and would no longer need to live in fear of the unknown and everything over which they had no control. It was all taken care of by a benevolent force, who was the greatest of all.

This applies easier to monotheism than to other forms of religion, but it can be traced in many mythologies and beliefs around the world. It also connects to James G. Frazer's idea that people in the past tried magic to control what could not be controlled by physical action, and when that failed, they turned to prayer and worship. The search for tools to handle the perils of life has been going on as far back as we can trace, and in every culture.

Of course, this strife is not limited to the threats of unpredictable fate, the workings of which are beyond our understanding. It is the same with the everyday difficulties of finding food, avoiding risks to our well-being, and so on. It's the struggle to survive.

We keep wrestling with our fears of the known as well as the unknown. We keep developing our tools — both those of evident use and those putting trust in superstition. As soon as a threat is defined, whether rightly or wrongly, we work on avoiding it and do not stop until we succeed. It is an urge that never leaves us.

Probably it is also the core incentive behind humans gathering into groups and continuing to expand and advance these groups into civilizations. We do it primarily to survive, secondarily to survive comfortably.

So far, it is only the ultimate threat that defies our efforts, also pointed out by Freud in his essay: There is no escaping death. We have succeeded in prolonging our life expectancy, especially during the last couple of centuries, but just by so much. We keep trying, with frenzy, by means of science as well as precautions on a personal level. But there is no changing the outcome. We can only postpone it, and even that is quite uncertain.

This has been known for as long as we have been conscious beings. If religion is born out of fear and the need for solace, death must be its major objective. We need to overcome the fear of it, or every life is one of panic increased by time, and we need solace afore the fact that death will come, no matter what.

Not that every mythology is doing a very good job at it, as discussed previously. In many of them, death is still to be dreaded, either because of what horrors await or because nothing is stated about it.

The two religions dealing substantially with the afterlife, Christianity and Islam, promise good tidings for the faithful. After death, people will get what they deserve, and for the believers the prospects are very promising. Might that have added to the successful spread of those two religions in the world? It has certainly always been a central element of their teaching and a central conviction among their believers.

This may also be the main reason for those religions keeping vast numbers of followers, in spite of scientific progress making those beliefs increasingly questionable. Freud's hope for the illusion coming to an end is yet to come true.

The simple fact that science cannot present the same solace, afore the bitter end of every life, is why it can't replace religion. What life is really like is not what we want it to be. So, a more attractive alternative — no matter how imaginary — is not easily abandoned.

Freud was aware of this, but he underestimated its persistence.

Civilization and Its Discontents

Three years after the above discussed book, in 1930, Freud published *Civilization and Its Discontents*, which deals with similar subjects. Its main perspective is not religion, but man's struggle with conforming to the demands of society. Freud finds, though, that religion plays a significant part in this dilemma.

The Oceanic Feeling
He begins by confessing that there is one aspect of religion, which he neglected in the previous book. It is the overwhelming feeling it can bring to its believers, "a sensation of 'eternity', a feeling as of something limitless, unbounded, something 'oceanic'."[57]

The observation is not his own, but was reported in a letter to him from an "exceptional" man, whom he does not name.[58] It was the French author Romain Rolland, with whom he corresponded for many years, in a letter dated December 5, 1927. Rolland spoke from personal experience, whereas Freud confesses that he cannot find that feeling in himself, which does not stop him from defining it:

> *So it is a feeling of indissoluble connection, of belonging inseparably to the external world as a whole.*[59]

He is jumping to conclusions. That oceanic feeling is a well-known phenomenon in many religions. For example, there is what in Christianity has long been called ecstasy, the trance induced by shamanic rites, and the concept of satori in Zen. But it can also be likened to the euphoria of the audience

---

[57] Sigmund Freud, *Civilization and Its Discontents* (*Das Unbehagen in der Kultur*), transl. Joan Riviere, London 1930, p. 8.

[58] J. Moussaieff Mason, *The Oceanic Feeling*, Dordrecht 1980, p. 34.

[59] Freud 1930, p. 9.

at a rock concert, or the inspiration bordering on possession that overwhelms some poets. It is the awe also atheists experience when watching nature at its most splendid.

That spectacular sensation is not exclusively religious, although it is understood as such when experienced in such a setting. Considering the characteristics of Freud's psychology, one would think he should compare it to the orgasm. But the closest he comes to that is seeing similarities to being in love.[60]

Instead, using his definition above, he connects that oceanic feeling to a mind unable to separate the inner world from the outer one. It's all one. That is the mind of an infant:

> *Originally the ego includes everything, later it detaches from itself the external world. The ego-feeling we are aware of now is thus only a shrunken vestige of a far more extensive feeling — a feeling which embraced the universe and expressed an inseparable connection of the ego with the external world.*[61]

He goes on to suppose that this primary ego conception is preserved in those people who experience the oceanic feeling. But he rejects the idea that it can be the cause of religion. Instead, he explains it as the child's longing for a protective father. Later in the book, to no surprise, Freud repeats his theory of the Oedipus complex, the guilt remaining after a primeval patricide.[62]

Civilization or Culture

But Freud's book is not aimed at investigating the cause and effect of religion. His scope is wider. As the title implies, it is about man's ambiguous relation to society as a whole. It protects the individual from potential malice of others — Freud

---

[60] Ibid., p. 10.
[61] Ibid., p. 13.
[62] Ibid., pp. 118ff.

compares it to the child's need of a good father[63] — but that also means the individual's own urges and impulses are restrained. That is what causes the discontent.

Freud's theories make frequent use of what he regarded as conflicting opposites, such as men's needs versus those of women, sons competing with their fathers, and personal impulses subdued by social norms. His focus here is the conflict between human nature and social order. The animalistic urges in men must be held at bay for civilization to appear and advance. Religion is one of the tools by which this is accomplished.

In other words, the conflict he explores is that between nature and civilization. But that polarity is somewhat flawed. The term civilization suggests an advanced society, where the population is *civilized*, traditionally also connected to the *city* and its particular demands on its *citizens*. These words are all etymologically connected, implying the difference between urban and rural.

The antonym to civilization would be something like barbarism or savagery, which is how Freud and many others at his time regarded people of the prehistoric past as well as indigenous tribes in the present. Another often used word was *primitive*. His comparison of the child's mentality vis-a-vis that of the adult points to the same idea of a development over time, which was seen as having been halted in the case of indigenous people.

It is the difference between the primitive and the advanced, which was believed to be an accurate division of societies. They were societies, all of them, but some were developed and others remained in sort of an infantile state. The latter are still often categorized as underdeveloped, as if the only development a society can have is towards modern industrialism.

That is definitely how Freud saw it, but his book is not

---

[63] Ibid., p. 21.

comparing different societies. The opposite it describes is that between the individual and the collective, in particular the natural urges of the former versus the cultural condition of the latter. The conflict is between instinctual and regulated behavior.

It is analogous to the expression made famous in the comic *Calvin and Hobbes* by Bill Watterson: "You can take the tiger out of the jungle, but you can't take the jungle out of the tiger." A wild tiger can be captured, but not tamed.

So, the fundamental opposition Freud discusses in his book is the one between human nature and human culture. The German word he uses already in the title is *Kultur*, culture, which is possible to interpret as civilization. But for that there is the German word *Zivilisation*, which he did not use even once in his book. The word *Kultur*, on the other hand, is used over 60 times.[64]

He presents the same definition of the concept as he used in *The Future of an Illusion*:

> *We will be content to repeat that the word 'culture' describes the sum of the achievements and institutions which differentiate our lives from those of our animal forebears and serve two purposes, namely, that of protecting humanity against nature and of regulating the relations of human beings among themselves.*[65]

That is a definition fitting neither culture nor civilization well. It lacks the complexity of what is meant by civilization, and it contains very little of what is included in the concept of culture. It is more appropriately applied to the word society.

Words have lives of their own, making fixed and exclusive definitions of them precarious. One difference between the concepts of civilization and culture, though vague, is that the

---

[64] Sigmund Freud, *Das Unbehagen in der Kultur*, Wien 1930.
[65] Freud, *Civilization and Its Discontents*, 1930, p. 49f.

former is about structure and the latter about content. Where civilization points to how a society is organized, culture is about how we act in it, what we do with it. Another interesting difference, relevant in the context of Freud's book, is that not all societies can be described as civilizations, but they are all cultures.

Freud's theory does not only concern the societies that have developed into what are called civilizations, but any human society demanding its individuals to adapt to it — and that is every society, whether ancient or contemporary, big or small, rural or urban. So, the English title of the book is slightly misleading.

Still, Freud seems to have approved the use of civilization instead of culture. In a letter to the translator Joan Riviere, he pondered other words in the title, suggesting it to be *Man's Discomfort in Civilization*. She was the one coming up with the wording that was adopted.[66]

There are additional complications with the title. It implies that some citizens are discontent, and accordingly others are not, as if immune. But in Freud's view on the human nature, it would be close to impossible for some to be completely content with the restrictions society puts on its members. There may be varied degrees of discontent, but it touches all. That is also what the German title, *Das Unbehagen in der Kultur*, implies — the discomfort, as Freud would have it in English, is universal.

The Pleasure of Conforming

Certainly, society's demands on people are straining. That goes for any society at any time, as well as every member of it. The world literature is full of examples, from the epic of Gilgamesh and on. Anthropological studies have shown the same in any culture examined. No mystery there.

---

[66] Sigmund Freud, *Civilization and Its Discontents*, transl. James Strachey, New York 1962, p. 6.

As for the causes to this conflict, though, answers are uncertain, to say the least. Sigmund Freud's contribution has not reached an end to the quest. The most intriguing question is why humans would at all form societies that discomfort them. Freud claims that it is to protect them from their own malice. They gang together so that they can overpower any one person among them who is a threat:

> *Human life in communities only becomes possible when a number of men unite together in strength superior to any single individual and remain united against all single individuals. The strength of this united body is then opposed as 'Right' against the strength of any individual, which is condemned as 'brute force'. This substitution of the power of a united number for the power of a single man is the decisive step towards civilization.*[67]

Freud's description of mankind is far from flattering. To him, man is a brutal beast against whom great measures are needed to avoid a bloodbath. He claims it is the major task of culture:

> *Culture has to call up every possible reinforcement in order to erect barriers against the aggressive instincts of men and hold their manifestations in check by reaction-formations in men's minds.*[68]

But a species needing that kind of protection from itself would not have survived. It cannot be the explanation, at least not the whole explanation.

Freud's analysis of this dilemma has one major flaw. It is based on the assumption that human urges are personal. They are not. There is no urge greater than that of being included

---

[67] Freud, *Civilization and Its Discontents*, 1930, p. 59.
[68] Ibid., p. 86.

and accepted among fellow humans. We may be beasts, but we are social beasts. That is at the core of our nature. So, the joy of inclusion vastly overtrumps the inconveniences of conforming. Actually, to any social beast, conforming is a pleasure, not an annoyance.

This basic animalistic tendency predates every religion and elaborate social structure. The extreme introverted perspective of psychoanalysis is probably what made Freud underestimate the social character of individual aspirations. We fulfill ourselves by the approval of others. It is so essential to our lives that we are even prepared to give up life itself for it.

Discussing the Jesus quote about loving one's neighbors as oneself, Freud states that "nothing is so completely at variance with original human nature as this."[69] He could not be more wrong. Compassion is embedded in human nature. We feel the pains and pleasures of others as if they were our own.

Freud's book claims that the discontent lies in the self-restraint of conforming to society, but that is joyous. The real discontent lies in not being able to conform completely. Individual satisfaction is bitterly unsatisfactory if perceived to be contrary to social demands and expectations. That is when the sense of guilt sets in — not when following the social norms, but when deviating from them.

That is where the theory of the Oedipus complex collapses. Sons joining to revolt against a father who is the oppressor of a whole tribe are not tormented by their action, but they would be if their fear hindered them from putting an end to that single man's dominance.

It is deeply rooted in the human nature that the interest of the collective surpasses that of any individual. When this is not upheld is when guilt sets in.

So, in Freud's Oedipus scenario, the sons would really have been utterly frustrated until they finally acted, and then at peace. They freed the tribe of a tyrant.

---

[69] Ibid., p. 87.

Consequently, such a patricide could never have been the origin of religion.

Moses and Monotheism

In *Moses and Monotheism*, which was published in 1939, the same year Freud died, he boldly repeats his theory about the origin of religion, although having received substantial criticism for it during the quarter-century since he first presented it.

If anything, he proclaims it with even less reservation, stating that his conviction "has only become stronger since." He continues:

> *From then on I have never doubted that religious phenomena are to be understood only on the model of the neurotic symptoms of the individual, which are so familiar to us, as a return of long forgotten important happenings in the primaeval history of the human family, that they owe their obsessive character to that very origin and therefore derive their effect on mankind from the historical truth they contain.*[70]

At least, he points out already with the title of his book that his speculations mainly concern monotheism. Still, as in the quote above, he keeps on claiming that his findings apply to all religion, and not just Judaism, Christianity, and Islam.

The Story of the Patricide

Freud gives a narrated form of the primeval event of the father murder, more explicit and detailed than in *Totem and Taboo*. He begins with the following reservation, which had only been vaguely implied in the previous book:

> *The story is told in a very condensed way, as if what in*

---

[70] Sigmund Freud, *Moses and Monotheism* (*Der Mann Moses und die monotheistische Religion*), transl. Katherine Jones, Letchworth 1939, p. 94.

reality took centuries to achieve, and during that long time was repeated innumerably, had only happened once.[71]

Certainly, it has the flavor and characteristics of a story — or a myth. Because of its fluent form, its added details compared to the version in *Totem and Taboo*, and its striking similarity to many myths, I repeat it below in its entirety,[72] inserting a few comments in between:

The strong male was the master and father of the whole horde: unlimited in his power, which he used brutally. All females were his property, the wives and daughters in his own horde as well as perhaps also those robbed from other hordes. The fate of the sons was a hard one; if they excited the father's jealousy they were killed or castrated or driven out.

Castration was not specified as a threat to the sons in *Totem and Taboo*, but in *Moses and Monotheism* it is mentioned also in relation to individual neurotic behavior, where Freud sees the fear of castration as a significant component. He continues his narrative:

They were forced to live in small communities and to provide themselves with wives by robbing them from others.

The robbing of wives was not mentioned in *Totem and Taboo*. Instead, it was implied that the outcast sons turned to homosexual relations among themselves and that this formed bonds between them, forging them together so that they found the courage to revolt against the father.

Moses and Monotheism gives no clue as to why this important ingredient in the bonding of the sons — also effective

---

[71] Ibid., p. 130.

[72] Ibid., pp. 130f.

in the society they form after their revolt — is now abandoned from his speculations.

> *Then one or the other son might succeed in attaining a situation similar to that of the father in the original horde. One favoured position came about in a natural way: it was that of the youngest son who, protected by his mother's love, could profit by his father's advancing years and replace him after his death.*

There is no mention of this fortunate opportunity of the youngest son in *Totem and Taboo*.

> *An echo of the expulsion of the eldest son, as well as of the favoured position of the youngest, seems to linger in many myths and fairy tales.*

In this book Freud refers rather frequently to myths, also using examples from the Bible, whereas in *Totem and Taboo* he referred almost exclusively to ritual and anthropological observations.

He finishes his account of the primeval patricide, with the added event of the father being devoured:

> *The next decisive step towards changing this first kind of "social" organization lies in the following suggestion. The brothers who had been driven out and lived together in a community clubbed together, overcame the father and according to the custom of those times all partook of his body.*

Freud also expands a little on the concept of a mother goddess and a hint of a matriarchy, partly related to the affection of the sons for their mother: "A good part of the power which had become vacant through the father's death passed to the women; the time of the matriarchate followed."[73] This matriarchy, he explains, was short-lived. A patriarchy returned, though not as potent as the original one.[74]

Collective Neurosis

In *Moses and Monotheism*, Freud expands and clarifies his theory somewhat. He specifies the stages gone through by mankind as a whole, comparing them to the individual neurotic stages of "early trauma — defense — latency — outbreak of the neurosis — partial return of the repressed material."[75]

The analogy makes additional sense, since he claims that "the genesis of the neurosis always goes back to very early impressions in childhood."[76] Also mankind's patricide supposedly took place at an early stage, a childhood in the development of the human species. He describes the process:

> *That is to say, mankind as a whole also passed through conflicts of a sexual-aggressive nature, which left permanent traces but which were for the most part warded off and forgotten; later, after a long period of latency, they came to life again and created phenomena similar in structure and tendency to neurotic symptoms.*[77]

The latency mentioned, existing both in the individual and the collective, is a sort of mental period of incubation, in which the traumatic event is forgotten to the conscious mind. But it remains unconsciously and gains strength, so that when it erupts, it is much more potent than it was at the time of the traumatic event:

---

[73] Ibid., p. 132.
[74] Ibid., p. 134.
[75] Ibid., p. 129.
[76] Ibid., p. 118.
[77] Ibid., p. 129.

> *It is specially worthy of note that every memory returning from the forgotten past does so with great force, produces an incomparably strong influence on the mass of mankind and puts forward an irresistible claim to be believed, against which all logical objections remain powerless very much like the* credo quia absurdum.[78]

He compares this phenomenon to the delusion in a psychotic person, having a long-forgotten core of truth that upon reemerging becomes both distorted and compulsive.[79]

Latency of Memories

As a consequence of this latency, Freud needs to explain how something forgotten can remain through generations, to emerge in people as a very vivid and powerful memory of sorts.

In *Totem and Taboo,* he supposed no forgetting of the patricide. On the other hand, he did not specify that the memory was kept through the generations. What was implied was an established totemism, containing the trauma of the patricide. This totemism continued to be obeyed, long after the actual event had been forgotten.

In *Moses and Monotheism,* he introduces *latency,* the suppressed memory able to reemerge, and therefore he needs to explain this process. Doing so, he comes strikingly close to Carl G. Jung's theories of the collective unconscious and the archetypes.

Freud states very clearly that people did forget, "in the course of thousands of centuries," about the initial patricide. So, how could that forgotten memory return? He uses the analogy with the individual, whose traumatic memory is repressed, buried deep in the unconscious, but has not disap-

---

[78]Ibid., p. 136. *Credo quia absurdum*: I believe because it is absurd.

[79]Ibid., p. 137.

peared. It can reemerge. When doing so, it has the same great force suggested about mankind as a whole. Both the individual and the collective have this ability:

> *I hold that the concordance between the individual and the mass is in this point almost complete. The masses, too, retain an impression of the past in unconscious memory traces.*[80]

Such repressed memories may emerge in certain circumstances. With collective memories, this is most likely to happen when recent events are similar to those repressed.[81]

Archaic Heritage
Freud goes on to speculate that the individual does not only have personal memories stored in the unconscious, but also "what he brought with him at birth, fragments of phylogenetic origin, an archaic heritage."[82]

He gives no explanation to how such a memory can be kept and transported through the generations, but finds support for it in observations of patients. When they react to early traumata, when an Oedipus or castration complex is examined, other than purely personal experiences seem to emerge. These make more sense if regarded as somehow inherited from earlier generations. Freud believes that they are part of what he calls the archaic heritage.

He also uses the argument of "the universality of speech symbolism,"[83] the ability to have one object symbolically substituted by another, which is particularly strong in children. This symbolism is also at work in dreams. Freud regards it as

---

[80]Ibid., p. 151.

[81]Ibid., pp. 152f.

[82]Ibid., p. 157. By *phylogenetic* Freud means something "pertaining to racial development." Ibid., p. 217.

[83]Ibid., p. 158.

an ability inherited from the time when speech was developing. He is rather vague here, giving no examples of what kinds of objects and symbols he refers to.

He admits that the science of biology allows no acquired abilities to be transmitted to descendants, but boldly states: "I cannot picture biological development proceeding without taking this factor into account."[84]

Here he makes a comparison to animals, which he regards as fundamentally not very different from human beings in this respect. The archaic heritage of the "human animal" may differ in extent and character, but "corresponds to the instincts of animals." What makes a memory enter the archaic heritage is if it is important enough or repeated enough times, or both. Regarding the primeval patricide, he is quite certain:

> *Men have always known in this particular way that once upon a time they had a primaeval father and killed him.*[85]

These theories have a striking resemblance to Jung's ideas of the collective unconscious and the archetypes. They even use similar arguments. Still, Freud makes no mention of Jung in the book, and no comparison with his models.

They were, of course, distanced since decades, and not on speaking terms — but Freud was aware of Jung's theories, which were well developed and widely known in the time of *Moses and Monotheism*. Freud must have recognized and pondered the similarities, but decided not to do so in writing.

Moses

Freud gives two examples from biblical events, on which to apply his theory — those of Moses and Jesus.

About Moses, Freud claims that he was not Jewish but an Egyptian, befriending a Jewish tribe. Moses brought this tribe

---

[84]Ibid., p. 160.

[85]Ibid., p. 161.

out of Egypt and converted it to his monotheistic religion, which was Pharaoh Ikhnaton's worship of the single sun god Aton.[86] It was introduced as the state religion of Egypt by the pharaoh in the 14th century BC. Soon after his demise, Egypt returned to its previous polytheism.

The reason for a monotheistic god at all appearing in an otherwise abundantly polytheistic culture, Freud finds in the imperialistic success of Egypt, immediately preceding the cult of Aton: "God was the reflection of a Pharaoh autocratically governing a great world empire."[87] Then Freud imagines a fate of Moses, similar to that of the primeval tyrant father:

> *The Jews, who even according to the Bible were stubborn and unruly towards their law-giver and leader, rebelled at last, killed him and threw off the imposed Aton religion as the Egyptians had done before them.*[88]

Freud readily admits to have picked up the idea of Moses being killed by the Jewish tribe from a 1922 text by the German theologian and biblical archaeologist Ernst Sellin.[89] Both Sellin's theory and Freud's interpretation of it have been questioned by scholars.

Later on, in Freud's account of events, this Jewish tribe met and joined with another. As part of the compromise between the tribes, they adapted the worship of a volcano-god Jahve, influenced by the Arabian Midianites.[90]

---

[86] Ibid., p. 41. Ikhnaton is usually spelled Akhenaton or Akhenaten, and accordingly Aton is often spelled Aten.

[87] Ibid., p. 105.

[88] Ibid., p. 98.

[89] Ernst Sellin, *Mose und seine Bedeutung für die israelitisch-jüdische Religionsgeschichte*, Leipzig 1922.

[90] Freud, *Moses and Monotheism*, p. 98. The Midianites are mentioned in Genesis 25:1-4 as descendants of Abraham's son Midian. Exodus 2:15-21

In an effort to release themselves of the guilt for having killed Moses, the tribe insists on proclaiming him the father of this new monotheistic religion. In that way, they almost accomplish the father worship, which is the basis of Freud's theory on the origin of religion. By time, Jahve transforms to be more and more like the Egyptian god Aton.[91]

Jesus
Freud moves on to compare the story of Moses to that of Jesus, who was also sacrificed — but willingly. According to Freud, this was a symbolic amends for a primeval patricide:

A Son of God, innocent himself, had sacrificed himself — and had thereby taken over the guilt of the world.[92]

Jesus was proclaimed the son of god, i.e., the symbolic foremost son of the murdered father, the leader of the rebellion. He shouldered the responsibility for the father's death and suffered the equivalent punishment for it. Thus, the other sons, the rest of mankind, could in their minds feel forgiven by the father.

This is a process reminding of the Greek concept of *catharsis*, a cleansing that brings relief. Though Freud does not mention catharsis in the book, he was not unaware of its relevance to therapy. Its psychological application was introduced by Freud's mentor Josef Breuer in the 1880's, who called it the cathartic method. It was discussed by both in a book from 1895.[93]

To Freud, this sacrifice is unavoidable, because "a growing feeling of guiltiness had seized the Jewish people — and

---

has Moses flee to the land of Midian, where he marries a daughter of the priest.

[91] Ibid., pp. 102f.

[92] Ibid., p. 139.

[93] Josef Breuer & Sigmund Freud, *Studies in Hysteria*, transl. A. A. Brill, New York 1936 (originally published in German 1895), p. v.

perhaps the whole civilization of that time — as a precursor of the return of the repressed material."[94]

To Freud, the primeval patricide is the true original sin. And to no surprise he sees the Holy Communion as an example of the totem feast, where the totem animal was ritually consumed.

Freud finds a significant difference in the fates of Moses and Jesus — the former being a father figure, the latter that of a son. Therefore, he sees the Mosaic religion as essentially focused on the father, whereas Christianity is focused on the son:

> *The old God, the Father, took second place; Christ, the Son, stood in His stead, just as in those dark times every son had longed to do.*[95]

Judeo-Christian Relevance

No doubt, Christianity has several elements leading to somewhat similar impressions as those suggested by Freud. There is a sacrificed prophet teacher who repeatedly refers to an omnipotent father figure, a ritual meal of the martyr's flesh and blood, et cetera. There is also the desperate cry on the cross:

"My God, my God, why hast thou forsaken me?"[96]

That would seem like a vindictive father. Jesus is quoting from Psalms 22 of the Old Testament, which describes a person in utter misery, despised and mocked by his fellow men, crying for God's aid but not getting it. He promises to praise God wide and loud if he gets saved. Psalms 22 doesn't reveal who asks the question or how that works out, but the desperate call for help and promise to repay it is nothing unfamiliar.

The killing and dividing of a primeval being is a common motif among creation myths. Oddly, it is not used as an example by Freud, although he must have come across such exam-

---

[94]Freud, *Moses and Monotheism*, pp. 138f.

[95]Ibid., p. 141.

[96] Matthew 27:46 and Mark 15:34, *King James Bible*.

ples in his studies of mythology through Frazer and others. On the other hand, it is also easy to find mythologies with little or no trace of such a beginning.

Freud's theory seems more plausible in the sphere of Judeo-Christian religion, where a sole high god with male traits is worshipped. In religions swarming with gods of both genders, the conclusion makes far less sense.

Freud's religion is a male one, which he readily admits already in *Totem and Taboo*: "In this evolution I am at a loss to indicate the place of the great maternal deities who perhaps everywhere preceded the paternal deities."[97] He suggests that maternal goddesses dominated prior to the patricide, but were substituted with a high father god as a result of it. That in turn led to society as a whole evolving into patriarchy. The fatherless state after the patricide was replaced by a new patriarch.

That would risk the whole thing happening all over. But Freud sees a difference in the new patriarchy:

> *Now there were patriarchs again but the social achievements of the brother clan had not been given up and the actual difference between the new family patriarchs and the unrestricted primal father was great enough to insure the continuation of the religious need, the preservation of the unsatisfied longing for the father.*[98]

Again, this chain of events is likelier, to say the least, in a society with a monotheistic religion, like the Judeo-Christian sphere. In *Moses and Monotheism*, he slightly altered his views on a mother goddess and a matriarchy, as mentioned above.

Guilt, too, is much more present in Judeo-Christian religion than in many others. This part of Freud's theory is even weaker than that about an actual battle between father and sons.

---

[97]Freud, *Totem and Taboo*, p. 246.
[98]Ibid.

The concept of guilt felt and punished for generations is expressed repeatedly in the Bible. But in a time preceding the Bible, as well as in cultures free of its influence, we have little to confirm such persistence and dominance of that emotion. Instead, history tells us that people did not have that much trouble ridding themselves of any guilt, even when performing worse acts than killing a tyrant father.

Certainly, there are emotions that torment all members of our species, and rule over many of our actions. But Freud fails to prove that guilt is one of them, outside of his own cultural frame of reference.

No Cure for Oedipus
In spite of its flaws, Freud's bold thesis gives food for thought. Certainly, sexuality, death, and the complications of blood relations appear as themes in countless myths — as they do just about constantly in our minds.

Several species, including mankind, are subject to lots of struggles in the process of reproduction. Males compete over the females, often violently. A strong male might not be satisfied by a first choice only, but would strive to exclude the other males completely from approaching the females. If any species were to find the solution of suppressed males joining and thereby overpowering the leader, this would most likely be mankind.

Freud's theory may be a plausible rendering of a primeval democratization of sorts among savages, allowing for more frequent and evenly distributed procreation. But it fails as a theory of the origin of religion, when tested on the great variety of beliefs and rituals around the world.

Not only that. Even in the highly unlikely case of the worship of a god stemming from an ancient need to make amends, the theory gives few tools for further understanding. It is a *fait-accompli*, a dead-end about which one can say little more than that it belongs to the past and therefore it can't be changed.

Freud is remarkably uninterested in finding some kind of

cure for it, a way for mankind out of this emotional prison. He is only interested in showing that the Oedipus complex at the root of it is omnipresent, if not omnipotent. It is his baby, and he protects it vigorously. In more ways than one, it is his religion.

The Individual Versus the Collective
Freud's theories about religion, ritual, and myth have added little to the research in those fields. In the literature on those subjects, his theories are mentioned in passing as oddities that would have been forgotten if they came from a lesser-known figure than the father of psychoanalysis.

Still, Freud's view may deserve additional considerations. Religion has been an integrated part of human life as far back as we can see, and the role it has played might need tools like those of Freud to be understood. It cannot be explained by instinct alone. The instruments of psychology and sociology need also be applied.

As for Freud, biology plays a significant part in his theory, which is unexpected coming from a psychologist. In his view, the human psyche — at least the male one — is driven by animalistic instincts and how they are expressed in matters of procreation. Man remains a primitive beast, a misfit in whatever culture he lives. Freud saw that as the main source to mental discomfort and illness.

In *Moses and Monotheism,* he makes the clear distinction between the individual and the collective perspective, stating that the psychopathology of human neurosis belongs to individual psychology, "whereas religious phenomena must of course be regarded as a part of mass psychology."[99]

This is evident in the structure and practice of most religions. They regulate how the individual should behave in order to comply with the demands of the group. In this way, religions are social laws, with the claim of having a higher than

---

[99]Freud, *Moses and Monotheism*, p. 117.

human justification. They are also, with their rituals and myths, instruments by which the individual gets some aid in adapting to them.

This function of religion, to which Freud was no stranger, is less likely to be adequately researched within the field of psychology, though, than for example in social anthropology, which deals with human behavior in the concrete setting of daily social life.

The Stubborn Mind

Several things about Sigmund Freud's theories on myth and religion are puzzling — most of all his persistence with them. He stuck with the idea of the Oedipal patricide as the explanation to religion, although heavily criticized and even ridiculed for it. He did not even consider other theories.

Also, he based his understanding of religion solely on the Judeo-Christian monotheism with a fatherly almighty at the top, although he was far from ignorant of so many other religions to which his assumptions just were not applicable. Furthermore, his perspective on religion and its causes was exclusively male, where women were just bystanders with no active part in it.

He had made up his mind about the matter already when writing *Totem and Taboo* in 1913, being in his fifties, and stuck with it until the end of his life in 1939. During that time, he presented no new evidence, nor did he succeed in convincing any experts in the field of religion — just his own disciples, and not even all of them. Nothing could change his mind or even make him nuance his claims. For a propagator of science and its vast importance to society, that is absurdly stubborn.

If he had psychoanalyzed himself, he must have concluded that he had serious father issues, causing his firm opinion. Well, according to biographers and some passages in his texts, he did to some extent study himself like he would a patient. Still, it led to nothing but his strengthened belief in his own explanations. His thoughts were clouded by his commitment to what he regarded as his unique discoveries, which he was certain to be worthy of praise. Presumably his judgment was also influenced by a complicated relation to his father, but that is outside the scope of this book.

His stubbornness seems to have been contagious. As will be seen in the following pages, most of his students were just as stubborn, sticking to their master's paradigm without no more evidence than he had. Although himself an atheist, Freud's teaching was to him and to his students akin to theology. Not to be questioned. Those who did, like most notably Carl G. Jung, were regarded as pariah.

That is strange behavior from people who regarded themselves as experts on the human psyche.

The Secret Committee

A flagrant example of Freudian efforts to silence critique and discard opposition within the movement was the so-called Secret Committee, the inner circle of Freud's most loyal followers.

What led up to it was that two prominent students of Freud, Alfred Adler and Carl G. Jung, started to deviate from his teaching. This is how he describes it in his autobiography:

> *In Europe during the years 1911-13 two secessionist movements from psycho-analysis took place, led by men who had previously played a considerable part in the young science, Alfred Adler and C. G. Jung. Both movements seemed most threatening and quickly obtained a large following.*[100]

He goes on to explain that they wanted to "escape" recognizing the importance of infant sexuality and the Oedipus complex, Jung by attempting the interpretation of "an abstract, impersonal and non-historical character" and Adler by tracing "the formation both of character and of the neuroses solely to men's desire for power and to their need to compensate for their constitutional inferiority."

Freud reacted strongly to their deviations, having none of it. When they went their own way, they were excluded from his movement, regarded as outcasts. His own version of what passed, though, was deceptively idyllic:

---

[100] Sigmund Freud, *An Autobiographical Study*, transl. James Strachey, London 1935 (originally published in 1925), p. 96.

> *The criticism with which the two heretics were met was a mild one; I only insisted that both Adler and Jung should cease to describe their theories as 'psycho-analysis'.*[101]

But calling them heretics, as if Freud's teaching was of divine origin, is presumptuous, to say the least. And by refusing to allow their theories in the science he was so proud of having introduced, he revealed that he regarded it as solely his possession.

But that is not how science works. Freud's intolerance was utterly unscientific.

He admits to having been accused of intolerance, but defends himself by mentioning several psychoanalysts who stayed loyal to him and his ideas. To him, this is proof that he could not be intolerant:

> *I can say in my defence that an intolerant man, dominated by an arrogant belief in his own infallibility, would never have been able to maintain his hold upon so large a number of intelligent people.*[102]

That can certainly be discussed. Whatever intelligence is, it is not always accompanied by wisdom, or for that matter by integrity. That was soon to be shown.

In 1912, when both Adler and Jung had deviated from the doctrine, Ernest Jones suggested in a letter to Freud what was to be the Secret Committee. Freud responded enthusiastically to the idea:

> *What took hold of my imagination immediately is your idea of a secret council composed of the best and most trustworthy among our men to take care of the further development*

---

[101] Ibid., p. 97.
[102] Ibid., p. 98.

of and defend the cause against personalities and accidents when I am no more.[103]

Although Freud was only in his fifties at the time, he was so preoccupied by his legacy that he repeated a few lines down in the same letter: "I daresay it would make living and dying easier for me if I knew of such an association existing to watch over my creation."

The whole thing had a scent of boyish adventure to it, which Freud was aware of from the start:

I know there is a boyish, perhaps romantic element too in this conception but perhaps it could be adapted to meet the necessities of reality.

That did not stop him from adding romantic elements to it. When the Secret Committee was formed, initially consisting of Ernest Jones, Sándor Ferenczi, Hanns Sachs, Karl Abraham, and Otto Rank, he gave each of them a golden ring with a select motif from Roman mythology. They met in Vienna in May 2013, committing to the secret task of protecting Freud's dogma. He told Ferenczi that he was very happy with his "adopted children."[104]

Alfred Adler's departure from the Freudian doctrine was frustrating to his colleagues as well as to Freud, but it was definitely Carl G. Jung's break that shook them the most — Freud in particular. He had regarded Jung as his successor, a crown prince of sorts, and felt evident affection for him.

It was mutual until it went sour, followed by the kind of bitterness and disappointment similar to the end of a love story. Their correspondence indicates that the break had much more to do with their personal relation than with scientific dis-

---

[103] Phyllis Grosskurth, *The Secret Ring: Freud's Inner Circle and the Politics of Psychoanalysis*, Reading 1991, p. 47.

[104] Ibid., p. 52.

agreements, though both avoided that angle of the issue in their public writing. The crescendo of their quarrel came with Jung's letter to Freud in December 1912, where he wrote:

> *If ever you should rid yourself entirely of your complexes and stop playing the father to your sons and instead of aiming continually at their weak spots took a good look at your own for a change, then I will mend my ways and at one stroke uproot the vice of being in two minds about you.*[105]

These insults thinly disguised as a peace offering, whether accurate or not about Freud's behavior, soon led to their definite separation. Still, neither of them would scorn the other publicly. Jung continued for some time to express praise for Freud in his writing, and the latter stayed silent but asked Sándor Ferenczi to write a critique of Jung's work. Freud did not do so until Jung had formally broken all his ties with the psychoanalytic movement, in 1914.

That year, Freud wrote two texts criticizing the psychological theories of both Adler and Jung: *On Narcissism* and *The History of the Psychoanalytic Movement*, initially published in German. He was not kind to his former crown prince. In the latter text, after mentioning that he had seen Jung as his successor, his words get harsher. He claims that he had made Jung give up "certain race prejudices which he had so far permitted himself to indulge."[106] That is a grave accusation, and rather uncalled for if he had made Jung change his mind. Why, then, bring it up? He continues:

> *I had no notion then that in spite of the advantages enumerated, this was a very unfortunate choice; that it concerned a person who, incapable of tolerating the authority*

---

[105] Ibid., p. 50.

[106] Sigmund Freud, *The History of the Psychoanalytic Movement*, transl. A. A. Brill, New York 1917 (originally published in German 1914), p. 35.

of another, was still less fitted to be himself an authority, one whose energy was devoted to the unscrupulous pursuit of his own interests.

Considering Freud's own behavior, the same could be said about him. Later in the text, he objects to Jung's continued use of the term psychoanalysis although he has deviated from Freud's theories:

I am naturally entirely willing to admit that any one has the right to think and to write what he wishes, but he has not the right to make it out to be something different from what it really is.[107]

But no person can own a science, nor dictate how it may progress. Freud regarded psychoanalysis as his property, which should never deviate from the paradigms he had set. Then it is no longer science, but dogma. The members of the Secret Committee as well as many other psychoanalysts were strangely blind to the absurdity of Freud's claim.

Nevertheless, Jung soon shifted to the expression *analytical psychology* for his approach to the science and its methods.

In 1919, on Freud's suggestion, Max Eitingon was added to the Secret Committee, which continued its covert work into the late 1920's, but not without some turmoil. In 1927, when Karl Abraham had died and Otto Rank had left, continued disagreements within it led to its dissolution.

The same year, though, it was reconstituted and given an official status as a governing body of the International Association of Psychoanalysis, no longer secret. It consisted of Freud's daughter Anna Freud, who had previously replaced Otto Rank, Eitingon, Ferenczi, Jones, and Johann van Ophuijsen. The only remaining members from 1912 were Ferenczi

---

[107] Ibid., p. 52.

and Jones.[108] In the early 1930's, Ferenczi got increasingly alienated, but he died in 1933 without having formally resigned. Then, out of the original committee, only Ernest Jones — the one who had come up with the idea of it — remained.

It is a strange story. The correspondence between Freud and the members of the committee is full of intrigue, insinuations, gossip, and slander. Frankly, it is a soap opera, way below what would be expected from men of science — but certainly not unique in such communities, though rarely as flagrant as here.

The members of the committee were just as anxious to please their master as he was craving their praise. The varying rivalry and hostility between them all, Freud included, dimmed their reason even on psychological matters. They lapsed into using their psychology as a weapon to harm each other.

In her book about the Secret Committee, Phyllis Grosskurth concludes:

The epic story of the Committee evokes Aristotelian pity and terror but, alas, the spectacle does not provide us with any healing catharsis. We are witnessing not actors on a stage but real people wreaking havoc on each other.[109]

It is no exaggeration to say that this behavior was the norm among these people, who were at the top of the psychoanalytical movement. That means it must have been approved and even encouraged by its authoritarian leader, Sigmund Freud. Those who were loyal to him conformed to it, as long as their loyalty remained. If he had opposed to it, so would they. He did not.

It may have been less blameworthy for scientists in other fields than his, who could excuse themselves for not having the

---

[108] Grosskurth 1991, p. 192.

[109] Ibid., p. 220.

knowledge to predict the effect. But as a psychologist, Freud could hardly claim to be unaware of the consequences of this mentality within his movement. There were more than enough warning signals of utter discomfort within his Secret Committee, not to mention those who were the targets of their scheming.

Freud's effort was to keep his science pure, by which he meant strictly committed to his ideas, but what it led to was making the whole thing stained — the movement as well as its scientific claims.

Freudians

This is a selection of significant authors on psychoanalytical subjects, admittedly following in Sigmund Freud's footsteps, who have written to some extent about myth and religion. It is unlikely to be complete, but covers his major direct students and others close in time to his active years, starting with Karl Abraham who connected with Freud in 1907 and ending with Erich Fromm, who never met Freud and gradually deviated from his doctrine.

He was not the only one to do so, among the writers examined here. Several did by time go their own way, either on some minor issues or so that it led to a definite break from Freud. The first "outcasts" were Alfred Adler in 1911 and Carl G. Jung in 1914. Adler did not write at length on mythology, which is why he is not included in this book, whereas Jung did so in such quantity and making such an impression that he needs to be covered in a coming separate book. Another writer on mythology who left the Freudian movement was Otto Rank. He did so in 1924.

As with Freud, the views of his followers are explored through the texts they wrote on myths and religion. Of their books discussed here, the earliest one is Franz Riklin's *Wishfulfillment and Symbolism in Fairy Tales* from 1908, translated to English in 1915, and the latest is Helene Deutsch's *A Psychoanalytic Study of the Myth of Dionysus and Apollo* from 1969.

After that, strictly Freudian treatments on mythology of any significance are hard to find.

Karl Abraham

Karl Abraham (1877-1925) was a German psychoanalyst with close bonds to Sigmund Freud since their first meeting in 1907. The respect was mutual. Ten years after Abraham's death Freud still held him in high esteem, according to an account from American psychoanalyst John M. Dorsey: "I asked the Professor to name his 'best pupil' and he replied promptly, 'Karl Abraham'."[110]

Abraham also cooperated for three years with Carl G. Jung in Zurich, at Eugen Bleuler's psychiatric clinic. That was where he was introduced to psychoanalysis. But after disagreements — and some rivalry — Abraham moved to Berlin in 1907 to start his own psychoanalytic practice.[111] He was the first German to do so.[112] He remained there until his death.

The inner circle of loyal Freudians, the so-called Secret Committee, which was formed in 1912, had Karl Abraham as one of its initial five members. His loyalty to Freud's ideas is blatantly evident in the book discussed below, *Dreams and Myths* from 1909, where Freud is referred to as an unquestionable authority on almost every page.

Dreams and Myths

As the title suggests, Abraham compares myths to dreams, regarding both their form and their content. As for dreams, he follows slavishly Freud's understanding of them in *The Interpretation of Dreams* from 1899. What he proposes in his own book is that the same method can be used for analyzing myths:

---

[110] John M. Dorsey, *An American Psychiatrist in Vienna, 1935-1937, and His Sigmund Freud*, Detroit 1976. (web.archive.org/web/20070626155735/ http://www.freud.org.uk/fmfaq.htm)

[111] Anna Bentinck van Schoonheten, *Karl Abraham: Life and Work, a Biography*, transl. Liz Waters, New York 2018, pp. 44ff.

[112] Franz Alexander et al., *Psychoanalytic Pioneers*, New York 1966, p. 2.

> *It will bring out the proof that Freud's teachings, in a wide sense, can be transferred to the psychology of myths, and are even qualified to furnish wholly new grounds for the understanding of the sagas.*[113]

It is an interesting perspective, worthy of exploring. Certainly, there are many similarities between dreams and myths. Both leave the rules of natural law way behind and include strange creatures and events, belonging far more to fantasy than to reality. One would spontaneously say that they are somehow linked. There may be similar processes behind their creation.

Censored Dreams

The dreams that Abraham speaks of, though, are Freudian. He claims, like his teacher, that all dreams are. That means they are in essence the result of wishful thinking: "There lies, at the bottom of every dream, a repressed wish in the unconscious."[114] In the dream it appears under disguise, so that the dreamer does not become aware of the true nature of that wish.

There is a mental function taking care of that. Abraham calls it the censor: "The censor does not permit the repressed idea expression by clear, unequivocal words, but compels it to appear in a strange dress."[115] Therefore, dreams bring nothing new, but a distorted version of waking state thoughts, reshaped according to the demands of this inner censor.

The censoring distortion of dreams is done by condensation, merging several elements into one or a few, and by what Freud calls displacement, where elements are shuffled like a

---

[113] Karl Abraham, *Dreams and Myths: A Study in Race Psychology* (originally published in German 1909), transl. William A. White, New York 1913, p. 3.

[114] Ibid., p. 5.

[115] Ibid., p. 43.

deck of cards. There is also a secondary elaboration, when the dreamer tries to recall or retell the dream:

If we seek to call a dream back to memory, especially when we are telling it to another person, the censor undertakes additional changes, in order to make the dream distortion more complete.[116]

The typical dream contains wishes that we would not admit when awake. "These wishes, common to many or to all mankind, we meet also in the myths."[117]

In a dream the suppressed wish can be fulfilled in a symbolic way. Furthermore, the most profound wishes in the human psyche are those remaining since childhood. So, dreams represent the fulfillment of repressed wishes, and the deepest roots of them lie in the childhood of the dreamer.[118]

To no surprise, Abraham uses the Oedipus myth as an example, claiming that it expresses a suppressed childhood wish of the death of a parent, "the son, for the most part dreams of the death of the father, the daughter of the death of the mother."[119] He compares it to the myths of Uranus and Cronus, who were in battle with their children.

These fundamentals in the dreams of children, remaining through life, are the same as for humankind and its evolution from primeval times, expressed in myths:

The myth is a fragment of the repressed life of the infantile psyche of the race. It contains (in disguised form) the wishes of the childhood of the race.[120]

---

[116] Ibid., p. 46.
[117] Ibid., p. 9.
[118] Ibid., p. 6.
[119] Ibid., p. 8.
[120] Ibid., p. 36.

A process similar to that of the censor also takes place with myths over time, as "a myth suffers gradual modifications in the different life periods of a race."[121]

It Is Always About Sex
The theme of the Oedipus myth and many others is to Abraham, as to Freud, one of sexuality in symbolic representation: "Sexual symbolism, I assert, is a psychological phenomenon of mankind in all places and times."[122]

To stress this further, Abraham quotes the German writer Rudolf Kleinpaul: "Man sexualizes everything."

Abraham meets criticism of the Freudian focus on seeing sexuality expressed in so much of human thought and fantasies, by stating the opposite: "The danger of underestimating appears to me to lie much nearer."[123]

He goes on to see sexual symbols just about everywhere in dreams as well as myths. In the case of the latter, he gives the example from Genesis, where the serpent, the seducer of Eve, is a symbol of the male member, and the apple with which Eve seduces Adam represents the fruitfulness of the woman.[124]

The blissful existence in Paradise before the fall is a childish wish. He quotes Freud: "Paradise is nothing but the mass phantasy of the childhood of the individuals."[125]

Of particular interest is the fact that Adam and Eve were naked and not ashamed. It is something we all dream of being, without scorn from others, Abraham states, again referring to Freud's book about dream interpretation.

Adults refrain from doing so, but "children take great

[121] Ibid., p. 48.
[122] Ibid., p. 14.
[123] Ibid., p. 18.
[124] Ibid., p. 20.
[125] Ibid., p. 37.

pleasure in showing themselves naked."[126]

As additional proof of human fixation with sexuality, he gives examples from language, such as the grammar in German and other tongues applying gender even to inanimate objects, or the sexual innuendo of numerous words and expressions, e.g., to plow, long, mast, needle, and narrow.[127] Abraham insists:

> *Through the most different kinds of human phantasy the same symbolism runs which in a very substantial part is sexual.*[128]

He moves on to apply this basic principle to the myth of Prometheus, who created man and then stole fire from the gods to give it to men.

Analyzing the myth, he leans on the German philologist and folklorist Adalbert Kuhn, "the founder of comparative mythology,"[129] and his book *Die Herabkunft des Feuers und des Gottertranks* (*The Descent of Fire and the Potion of the Gods*) from 1859, with a second edition in 1886 simply called *Mythologische Studien* (*Mythological Studies*). Kuhn used linguistic comparisons of German names and terms to Vedic ones, and their ancient meanings.

But Abraham also sees immediate links to sexual symbolism in the plots of myths, such as Prometheus's gift to mankind of fire. He points out how fire was created in primeval times:

> *The primitive means of producing fire consisted of a stick of hard wood and a piece of soft wood which contained a hollow. Through turning and boring movements of the*

---

[126] Ibid., p. 38.
[127] Ibid., pp. 15ff and 21.
[128] Ibid., p. 27.
[129] Ibid.

stick in the hole the wood was set on fire.[130]

The analogy between that process and sexual intercourse is not very far-fetched. Abraham also mentions that the two parts of this primitive way of making fire often have the names of the male and female genitals, for example in Semitic languages: "In Hebrew the expression for male and female signifies exactly the borer and the hollowed."[131]

As for fire itself, it is that of the sun in the sky coming and going daily, lightning striking earth from above, and also the fire of life, which is the inner bodily warmth of every living human: "So long as it dwells in the body the body is warm. And like every fire the life-fire also goes out."[132]

Several ingredients in the myth point to Prometheus as creator of humankind, meaning that we would have a divine origin. And that is far from unique in mythology. It is a sign of human claim of grandeur:

Every race has associated the beginning of their existence with a myth, which reminds us in a surprising way of the delusions of descent of the insane. Every race will descend from its god head, be "created" by him. Creation is nothing but procreation divested of the sexual.[133]

By claiming such an elevated origin, we foster the idea of ourselves being divine: "If man is generated by god then is he, also, godly or the god is human. Man identifies himself then with the godhead."[134] Abraham points out that this is also suggested in Genesis, where God creates man after his image.

---

[130] Ibid., p. 28.
[131] Ibid., p. 30.
[132] Ibid., p. 29.
[133] Ibid., p. 41.
[134] Ibid., p. 42.

He compares the Prometheus myth to that of Moses. One brought fire and the other law. The sexual innuendo is found in the rod, "this always recurring symbol in numerous sagas."[135] Moses used his to strike water from the rock. "The symbolic significance of this staff becomes still clearer, when we recall, that it changed into a serpent before the eyes of Pharaoh."[136] The transformation of the staff means the return of the phallus to the quiescent condition.

Another biblical figure compared is Samson, who lost his power with his hair, and who in turn relates to Hercules:

> *Samson, as can be seen from the etymology of his name, is the sun god of the old Semitic heathendom and corresponds to Hercules of the Indo-Germanic saga.*[137]

Myths express a wish, which is hidden behind symbols because we don't want to confess it, even to ourselves: "It is always a wholly unsophisticated wish!"[138] The content of a more refined intellectual nature, such as ethical or religious morals of the myth, are later revisions: "I conceive the ethical-religious constituents of the myth as later impressions, as products of repression."[139]

In the case of Prometheus, as in just about every myth, the wish is a sexual one about the potency to procreate. It is described as an exclusively male ability, as if women had no significant part in it:

> *The Prometheus saga, in its oldest form, had the tendency to proclaim the masculine power of procreation as a prin-*

---

[135] Ibid., p. 51.

[136] Ibid., p. 66.

[137] Ibid., p. 52.

[138] Ibid., p. 58.

[139] Ibid., p. 69.

ciple of all life. That is the sexual delusion of grandeur of all mankind even to the present day.[140]

It is indeed likely that ancient ideas of procreation were that the seed from the man impregnated the woman, as if she were nothing more than a vessel. Man's semen was regarded as the seed, which is the meaning of the word, and woman was the fertile ground where it was sowed.

It is highly doubtful, though, that the same misconception was the rule also when Karl Abraham wrote his book. When Oskar Hertwig published his observations of sperm and egg fusion in the sea urchin in 1876,[141] it did not come as much of a surprise, and after it the understanding of the importance of both cells was well established. Other aspects of masculine delusions of grandeur, though, have been more persistent.

Abraham goes on to describe the mythological ambrosia or nectar of the gods in Greek mythology, which has a parallel in the Vedic *soma*. He sees them as representations of semen. In the repression of sexual content in the saga, "the semen gradually becomes transformed into the nectar of the gods."[142]

Abraham sees the repressed wish in disguise not only in myth, but in religion as such: "The wish theory of myths is amplified without difficulty to a wish theory of religion."[143] Man identifies with his god. In the monotheistic religions, though, this has in a process of repression become a belief in a caring-for father and the Madonna cult created a caring-for mother. Also, the belief in life after death is nothing but the fulfillment of a wish phantasy.

---

[140] Ibid., p. 62.

[141] Oscar Hertwig, "Beiträge zur Kenntniss der Bildung, Befruchtung und Theilung des thierischen Eies" (Contributions to the Knowledge of the Formation, Fertilization, and Division of the Animal Egg), *Morphologisches Jahrbuch*, volume 1, Leipzig 1876, pp. 347-434.

[142] Abraham, *Dreams and Myths*, p. 68.

[143] Ibid., p. 71.

Myths May Mean what They Say

There is little dispute about the wide presence of sexuality in the human mind and culture. The question is why it would be so elaborately repressed and replaced by more or less obvious symbols of it. This view speaks less of the long history of humankind than of the social norms of the early 20th century Europe in which Abraham wrote his book.

Humans reproduce, as do all the animals. This has never been a secret, nor the manner in which it is done and the urges involved. Although European society at the time of Karl Abraham repressed the expression of sexuality and sexual urges, it is quite doubtful that the same could be said about Greece when the myth of Prometheus took form, or myths of other cultures in other eras.

It is much more likely that the fire Prometheus brought was just fire and his creation of man was just the creation of man. The myth could very well express what it claims to express, which is an inventive fictional way of explaining how our species emerged and how we got the tool of fire. The pattern is easily recognizable from many myths of creation.

One could even toy with the idea that Prometheus's theft of fire from the gods was a fanciful version of one tribe stealing it from another in primeval times, before everyone knew how to make it. The tribe that was bereft of fire would be in an avenging mood, even if the theft was not of fire but merely the technique to ignite it.

In any case, assuming a myth to mean something altogether else than what it tells, demands much more evidence than linguistic association and the fact that we are quite obsessed by our sexuality. The light and warmth of fire is in itself something of tremendous importance to humankind since we learned how to create it at will.

Then there is the anomaly of so many Greek and other myths of old, dealing much more outspokenly with sexuality. The Greek gods were not discreet, nor were numerous deities of other mythologies. If Abraham's thesis would be correct, then all myths would have been censored and their sexual content suppressed. To name but a few, Zeus's transformation into a swan to seduce Leda, Poseidon's rape of Demeter and Medusa, and Pasiphaë's mating with a bull would have been hidden behind layers of symbolic alterations. That is certainly not the case.

But the relation between dreams and myths remains an interesting one, though not necessarily from a primarily psychoanalytical perspective.

The fact that we dream, and most likely have done so since at least the dawn of the human species, is surely a contributing factor to our creation of myths. Maybe many of the myths originated in the oral sharing of dreams and daydreams. That would be enough to explain the fantastic ingredients and absurd events of myths. Our dreams have a reality of its own, still today unbound by the laws of physics and immune to reason.

The mere fact that we in our heads can experience chains of events that have no outer existence is the prerequisite of any kind of storytelling.

Otto Rank

Another member of Freud's Secret Committee of his most loyal supporters was Otto Rank (1884-1939) — from its formation in 1912 until 1924, when Rank went his own way. Rank was born in Vienna, Freud's hometown, and joined with him already at the age of 21, in 1906. He remained a very close and appreciated collaborator for almost 20 years.

His literary debut was with *The Artist* in 1907, which presented a psychoanalytical perspective on artists. That continued to be one of his favorite themes, along with finding psychoanalytical patterns in myths.

Already in 1906, he was hired as a secretary for the Psychological Wednesday Society, later renamed the Vienna Psychoanalytic Society, although he still lacked a university degree.[144] Encouraged by Freud, he reached his PhD with *The Lohengrin Saga* in 1911.

That was the very first dissertation to apply a psychoanalytical method.

It was with his 1924 book *The Trauma of Birth* that he fell out of grace with Freud and his group of psychoanalysts. They criticized the book for deviating from Freudian dogma. Rank left the organization and Vienna, moving first to Paris and later to the USA. He died at the age of 55 in 1939, just a month after the death of Sigmund Freud.

The Birth of the Hero

In 1909, Otto Rank published *The Myth of the Birth of the Hero*, where he went through a number of myths, fairy tales and ancient works of fiction to extract a common pattern regarding the birth and emergence of hero figures. He found this:

---

[144] Dan Merkur, *Psychoanalytic Approaches to Myth: Freud and the Freudians*, New York 2005, p. 20.

The standard saga itself may be formulated according to the following scheme:

The hero is the child of most distinguished parents; usually the son of a king. His origin is preceded by difficulties, such as continence, or prolonged barrenness, or secret intercourse of the parents, due to external prohibition or obstacles. During the pregnancy, or antedating the same, there is a prophecy, in form of a dream or oracle, cautioning against his birth, and usually threatening danger to the father, or his representative. As a rule, he is surrendered to the water, in a box. He is then saved by animals, or by lowly people (shepherds) and is suckled by a female animal, or by a humble woman. After he has grown up, he finds his distinguished parents, in a highly versatile fashion; takes his revenge on his father, on the one hand, is acknowledged on the other, and finally achieves rank and honors.[145]

Later in the book he gives the pattern a more comprised form:

Summarizing the essentials of the hero myth, we find the descent from noble parents, the exposure in a river, and in a box, and the raising by lowly parents; followed in the further evolution of the story by the hero's return to his first parents, with or without punishment meted out to them.[146]

In the hundred pages of the book, Rank goes through a number of hero myths, also some fairy tales and fictional accounts, from the Babylonian king Sargon to Lohengrin. Among the many heroes are Moses, Oedipus (of course), Paris of

---

[145] Otto Rank, *The Myth of the Birth of the Hero: A Psychological Interpretation of Mythology* (*Der Mythus von der Geburt des Helden: Versuch einer psychologischen Mythendeutung*, 1909), transl. F. Robbins and Smith Ely Jelliffe, New York 1914, p. 61.

[146] Ibid., p. 68.

Homer's *Iliad*, Perseus, Hercules, Romulus, Jesus, and Tristan of the epic poem by Gottfried of Strasbourg. Several of them fit right into Rank's structure, whereas for others he sometimes has to argue elaborately.

The most strained of those arguments is when he uses Freud's theory about reversal to claim that an account of events may be interpreted as its opposite.[147]

Though sketching a few theories of explanation to this pattern of the hero myths, Rank is not interested in that aspect, nor does he care much for trying to trace the origin of the hero myth:

> *Of course no time will be wasted on the futile question as to what this first legend may have been; for in all probability this never had existence, any more than a 'first human couple.'*[148]

Instead, he concentrates on how the pattern and its ingredients should be understood from a psychoanalytical standpoint, much like Karl Abraham did in *Dreams and Myths*, which was published the same year and referred to in Rank's text.[149] Rank uses similar arguments and also finds his major source in Freud's book on dream interpretation. He defines the myth as a dream of the masses of the people.[150]

Myths are expressions of human imagination, especially that of the childish mind since "this imaginative faculty is found in its active and unchecked exuberance only in childhood."[151] Therefore, Rank argues, the myths mainly express the psychological urges of children, also those of psychoneu-

---

[147] Ibid., p. 75.
[148] Ibid., p. 4 (footnote).
[149] Ibid., p. 7.
[150] Ibid., p. 6.
[151] Ibid., p. 62.

rotic adults, who are shown by the teachings of Freud to have remained children, in a sense.[152]

In these adults, the childish emotions are preserved and exaggerated, which make them easier to analyze than the somewhat chaotic minds of children. So, the child inside the adult is revealed by the myth he composes:

> *Myths are, therefore, created by adults, by means of retrograde childhood fantasies, the hero being credited with the myth-maker's personal infantile history.*[153]

The mentally healthy adults, on the other hand, leave the childish sentiments behind, at least for the most part, to break free of the parents and form their own lives. But it is a straining process:

> *The detachment of the growing individual from the authority of the parents is one of the most necessary, but also, one of the most painful achievements of evolution.*[154]

In the mind of the child, though, the relation to the parents is one of affection leading to rivalry from feeling neglected. The child is upset for not constantly receiving the entire love of the parents. In hero myths, when the hero kills a powerful man standing in the way of his joining with his true love, he "kills in him simply the man who is trying to rob him of the love of his mother: namely the father."[155]

Nourishing the idea of being a step-child or adopted, "usually under the influence of story books,"[156] brings the

---

[152] Ibid., p. 63.
[153] Ibid., p. 82.
[154] Ibid., pp. 63f.
[155] Ibid., p. 77.
[156] Ibid., p. 65.

child some relief. Echoing Freud's view on the sexes, Rank sees this tendency more prominent in boys than in girls: "The imaginative faculty of girls is possibly much less active in this respect." To no surprise, he presents no evidence of it.

The child's conception of not living with its real parents is fed by a wish to replace them:

> *The entire endeavor to replace the real father by a more distinguished one is merely the expression of the child's longing for the vanished happy time, when his father still appeared to be the strongest and greatest man, and the mother seemed the dearest and most beautiful woman.*[157]

Rank calls it an example of family romance, and sees in it the link between the ego of the child and the hero myth, which explains "the unanimous tendency of family romances and hero myths."[158] Myths mirroring this childish idea have two parental couples — the biological ones and the step-parents — but they are really identical.

When puberty approaches, an element of ambition emerges in the child, with the wish to replace the parents who are now despised with others of a higher social rank.[159] This is also shown in the pattern of the hero myth, where his hostility is mainly targeted at the father.[160] The hero's rebellion against the father is explained as inevitable, often even commendable. That becomes an excuse for the revolt against the father in general, a relief of which the individual is in dire need: "This revolt had burdened him since his childhood, as he had failed to become a hero."[161]

---

[157] Ibid., p. 67.
[158] Ibid., p. 68.
[159] Ibid., p. 65.
[160] Ibid., p. 74.
[161] Ibid., p. 82.

Rank ends his text by comparing the hero myth to the mentality of the anarchist, claiming that "every revolutionary is originally a disobedient son, a rebel against the father."[162] The anarchist may follow in the footsteps of the hero when persecuting or even killing a king, but for both the true motivation can be questioned:

> *As the hero is commended for the same deed, without asking for its psychic motivation, so the anarchist might claim indulgence from the severest penalties, for the reason that he has killed an entirely different person from the one he really intended to destroy, in spite of an apparently excellent perhaps political motivation of his act.*[163]

One Can Dream

Certainly, there are many similarities between all kinds of myths from different times and cultures, whether they tell a hero's story or not.

There are also differences. Not even all the myths Rank lists in his book have the set of patterns he claims to be true for hero myths.

In spite of that, he makes no particular effort to explain why some of those myths lack one or more of those ingredients. Nor is he completely convincing when he argues for similarities where a reader must initially doubt them.

In his eagerness to point out psychological significances according to the Freudian doctrine, he is quick to allow things to represent something other than what meets the eye. For example, he explains the frequent event of a baby put in some vessel in a river or lake:

> *The exposure in the water signifies no more and no less than the symbolic expression of birth. The children come*

---

[162] Ibid., p. 93.
[163] Ibid., p. 94.

> *out of the "water." The basket, box or receptacle simply means the container, the womb.*[164]

In an accompanying footnote he adds that the box is in some myths represented by a cave, which also symbolizes the womb. As symbols go, they are quite obvious, but they raise the question why a baby, already born, would go through such a reenactment. To explain this, he actually uses Carl G. Jung. In 1909, when Rank published his text, Jung had not yet become persona non grata among the Freudians.

According to Jung, he explains, this mythical component is "the fantasy of being born again, to which the incest motive is subordinated."[165] This wish of returning to the mother's womb and rebirth from it is something Jung wrote about more than once. Still, it is strange that a baby would need that rebirth process. In the paradoxical worlds of myths and dreams, it would be just as plausible to have a grown man go through it — and that would make more psychological sense.

Some of Rank's patterns of hero myths are uncontroversial, such as the very common theme of a boy from meager circumstances growing up to get the princess and half the kingdom. Countless fairy tales tell the same story. No mystery there. Anyone who was not already from birth blessed with these fortunes would be charmed by the prospect. There is no psychological need for it to be an expression of father-envy.

Simply put, a much wider audience would find it easier to identify with a hero born into poverty than one already vastly privileged from the start. The privileged have always been a minority, or it wouldn't be a privilege.

The same thing can be said for the plot of the commoner child revealed to be of utter nobility. It is a dream scenario in no need of a deeply frustrated relation to one's parents.

The frequent recurrence of those motifs is not more of a

---

[164] Ibid., pp. 69f.
[165] Ibid., p. 83.

mystery than that we love to hear about someone winning the lottery but don't care much about one losing — although the latter is so much more common than the former.

The frequency in myths of a child abandoned by the parents, whether it is in a box on the water or in another manner, may seem peculiar at first, but it is tragically far from unheard of in real life. Through history, a multitude of children have been deserted by their parents, for different reasons and with different degrees of cruelty. It was a familiar occurrence to people of the past and sadly still is. A story aiming to describe the path from destitution to exaltation was likely to start with an abandoned child, so as to begin with utter misery.

In order to attract its audience, a story needs to work with extremes. Who cares about a prince growing up to be king, or a rich man's son inheriting the riches? It is what they do. But when a pauper gets to be king or a beggar strikes gold — that raises our eyebrows and our hopes, although we know it to be oh, so rare. We foster dreams about success because we would like to succeed. There is no hidden message to it.

What remains is the question of the hero's return to the original parents, either to elevate or to condemn them. It can easily be understood as tying the knots of the story.

If the hero was abandoned by his parents in the beginning of the story, the audience would want to know what happened to them. If they treated their child cruelly, we would expect vengeance. But if they left their child out of unfortunate necessity, we want reconciliation. It is for the sake of completing the story, and not an expression of some unconscious dynamics between children and parents.

Rank's psychoanalytical approach to hero myths is not implausible, but improbable compared to the primary principles of a narrative. A story has its own necessities and mechanics that should not be neglected in the analysis of it. When that has been considered, little remains to justify the psychoanalytical explanation of it.

Although Rank's conclusions about the hero myth have

their flaws, he must be credited for being so early among the psychoanalysts to pay attention to it and recognizing its significance. Later, it would be the archetype of central importance to Jung, and after that even more famously of Joseph Campbell.

The Interpretation of Dreams

The outstanding evidence of Freud's great appreciation of Otto Rank was that he allowed his apprentice to contribute to a new edition of *The Interpretation of Dreams*, which was Freud's major work. The 4th edition, published in 1914, contains two texts by Rank and even credits him as a co-writer of the book. The two chapters written by Rank are "Dreams and Poetry" and "Dreams and Myth."[166]

When Rank fell out of Freud's grace after deviating from his doctrine in the mid-1920's, it was proven by the same chapters being omitted from the following edition of the book — the 8th, released in 1930 — without any explanation. They have not reappeared in the book since. Below, a translation of the two texts from the 7th edition of 1922 is used.

Dreams and Poetry

The first of those texts, "Dreams and Poetry," starts by comparing dreams to the creation of poetry, stating that there are "deeper connections between the exceptional abilities of 'sleepers' and the 'inspired' soul."[167] Rank then uses a bundle of quotes mainly from poets to show their inklings of the functions and meanings of dreams in ways similar to Freud's doctrine. It is their poetic inspiration leading them to these realizations:

---

[166] Lydia Marinelli & Andreas Mayer, *Dreaming by the book: Freud's interpretation of dreams and the history of the psychoanalytic movement*, transl. Susan Fairfield, New York 2003 (originally published in German 2002), pp. 191f.

[167] Otto Rank, "Dreams and Poetry," Marinelli & Mayer 2003, p. 193.

> *All these insights into the nature of dreams, which we have combined into a dream theory close to the psychoanalytic conception, are actually just incidental by-products of the intuitive psychic knowledge that the poet displays artistically in his creations.*[168]

By this somewhat haphazard method, Rank claims to find poets confirming a number of Freudian principles: wish-fulfillment, dreams as guardians of sleep, dream mood change through reversal of affect, suppressed erotic impulses, secret wishes suppressed in childhood, the Oedipus complex and its incest fantasy, and even the strange concept of reversal.

In the last case he takes support from the Swedish author August Strindberg, quoting him about the theosophist notion that things observed from the astral plane look upside down: "That is why dreams are often to be interpreted *in reverse*, through antiphrasis, and in *Swedenborg* there is an indication of this perverted way of seeing things."[169]

Rank takes evident delight in this support from Strindberg, and from others, for Freudian dream analysis:

> *It is especially fascinating for the psychoanalyst to see for himself how dreams presented as poetry or in poetry are constructed according to the laws that have been established empirically and stand before psychoanalytic observation as actually experienced dreams.*[170]

He also touches on the link between daydreams and the creative artistic process. He sees them as an intermediate area between the dream world and poetry. While the daydreams correspond to undistorted dreams, truthfully revealing uncon-

---

[168] Ibid., p. 205.
[169] Ibid., p. 200.
[170] Ibid., p. 207.

scious cravings, the poems in their edited and adjusted forms are idealized versions.[171]

The primary problem with his speculations lies in the method of gathering quotes from the veritable cornucopia of our literary history. From such an abundance of material it is easy to find confirmations for just about any theory — or dismissal of it.

Standing out from the minds of the poets is not so much the meanings of dreams as their meaninglessness. Actually, this is something dreams are said to share with life as a whole. Shakespeare has Prospero say in *The Tempest*: "We are such stuff as dreams are made on, and our little life is rounded with a sleep."[172] Edgar Allan Poe agrees:

All that we see or seem
Is but a dream within a dream.[173]

So did, famously, with a particular twist, the Chinese Taoist Chuang Tzu in the 4th century BC, when waking up from dreaming he was a butterfly. He was not sure if it was he who had dreamt about being a butterfly, or a butterfly now dreaming of being him.[174] Chuang Tzu goes on to insist that there must be a difference, and calls it "the Transformation of Things."

Poe, too, had his ideas about the true nature of dreams and their relation to what we call reality:

I believe man to be in himself a Trinity, viz. Mind, Body,
and Soul; and thus with dreams, some induced by the

---

[171] Ibid., p. 218.

[172] William Shakespeare, *The Tempest*, Act IV, Scene I.

[173] Edgar Allan Poe, "A Dream within a Dream," J. H. Whitty, *The Complete Poems of Edgar Allan Poe*, Boston 1917, p. 123.

[174] James Legge, *The Sacred Books of China: The Texts of Taoism*, part 1, Oxford 1891, p. 197.

mind, and some by the soul. Those connected with the mind, I think proceed partly from supernatural and partly from natural causes; those of the soul I believe are of the immaterial world alone.[175]

August Strindberg, quoted by Rank on the reversal of dreams, wrote a whole play as if consisting of a dream, simply called *The Dream Play*. In a short introduction to it, which he called "A Reminder," Strindberg explains to have imitated "the disconnected but seemingly logical form of the dream."[176] He continues:

Anything may happen; everything is possible and probable. Time and space do not exist. On an insignificant background of reality, imagination designs and embroiders novel patterns: a medley of memories, experiences, free fancies, absurdities and improvisations.

That does not leave much room for a psychoanalytical interpretation to claim having the definite answer.

Dreams and Myth

Rank's second chapter, "Dreams and Myth," is a mere 17 pages and does little more than repeat what he and Karl Abraham had stated about the psychology of myths, as discussed above.

He begins by declaring that dreams are significant for the formation of myths and fairy tales.[177] That would necessarily make myths as personally specific as dreams are, but Rank

---

[175] Edgar Allan Poe, "An Opinion on Dreams," originally published in *Burton's Gentleman's Magazine*, August 1839. J. H. Whitty, *The Complete Poems of Edgar Allan Poe*, Boston 1917, p. lxiii.

[176] August Strindberg, "The Dream Play," *Plays by August Strindberg*, transl. Edwin Björkman, New York 1912, p. 24.

[177] Otto Rank, "Dreams and Myth," Lydia Marinelli & Andreas Mayer, *Dreaming by the book*, p. 221.

then speaks of a folk psychology creating myths from a culturally shared history and symbolism. There is "a genetic perspective that allows us to conceive of myths as the distorted remnants of wishful fantasies of entire nations, as it were the secular dreams of mankind in its youth."[178] Still, it is all rooted primarily in the personal relation to parents, sexuality, and the Oedipus complex.

For some myths, this relation is near at hand, but less obvious in other cases. To Rank it means that the myth has been distorted. As an example of this, he mentions the widespread "brother tales," which simply substitute the brother for the father in the same old Oedipal rivalry. But then there are brother tales where one avenges the other. That would be an anomaly, but Rank explains it:

> *Comparative myth research, in connection with the psychoanalytic mode of observation, makes it possible to uncover, from the heavily distorted versions in which the brother appears as his brother's avenger, a continuous chain of links to less distorted versions in which one brother removes another in order to win the latter's woman.*[179]

The explanation is as convenient as it is questionable. He gives no example of how the tale of an avenging brother would really be such a rivalry, when stripped bare. He is wise not to try. The rivalry between brothers is not unheard of in any culture — nor is the loyalty to the death between them. There is not just one way in which their relation could play out, either in their unconscious wishes or in real life.

Rank also touches on creation myths, which he regards from a psychoanalytical perspective as "infantile sexual curiosity concerning birth processes and its attempts, projected

---

[178] Ibid., p. 230.

[179] Ibid., p. 230.

onto the universe, to attain knowledge."[180] Then certainly the common creation myth motif of world-parents killed by their son reflects "all the ur-motifs of the infantile Oedipus complex in a wider sense."

The influence between dreams and myths is reciprocal. Rank mentions the psychoanalytical experience that people's dreams may make use of familiar themes from fairy tales:

There are dreams whose function is to depict current psychic manifestations of certain fairy-tale themes known from childhood.[181]

This points out the problem of the chicken and the egg as applied to dreams and myths. Like so much in the complexity of human thought and interaction, it is not a one-way street. So, there is not much point in trying to find one sole origin — just like it is pointless, according to Rank, trying to find the first human beings.

In a humble footnote Rank states something of fundamental importance, unfortunately without expanding on it. Discussing *Aethiopica* by Heliodorus, where Thyamis has a dream right when the rooster crows, Rank explains: "Dreams toward morning were held to be true."[182]

That is the hypnopompic state of lucid dreaming at the moment of waking up, which is discussed in the chapter about Erich Fromm. Psychoanalysts should really ask themselves if not these types of dreams are the only ones to which they have ever had access. Since we are unable to remember dreams without waking up from them, maybe those we do remember are all created more or less by the conscious mind at the process of waking up.

---

[180] Ibid., p. 231.
[181] Ibid., p. 237.
[182] Ibid., p. 232, footnote.

The Trauma of Birth

In 1924 Otto Rank released the book that would exclude him from Freud's entourage and soon also from Freud's support — *The Trauma of Birth*, where Rank claimed the experience of birth to be the first and foremost human trauma. Thereby, he dethroned the Oedipus complex from that position, albeit indirectly. So, the reaction from Freud and his loyal followers was no surprise.

It was a surprise to Rank, though, judging from the explicit and repeated reverence he shows Freud in the book. It is close to worship. He ends his preface by humbly declaring that "we owe to the instrument of investigation and to the way of thinking which Freud has given us in Psychoanalysis."[183] Through the text, Freud is praised for his "power of observation," which is "brilliant," "keen," and "clear," as is his thought. His accomplishment is "stupendous," his objectivity is "remarkable," and his discovery has "courage."[184]

Although Rank's theory of the birth trauma contradicts Freud's doctrine to quite some extent, he never even once states so, nor does he raise any other objection to Freud's ideas. He refers to Freud's theories and discoveries as nothing less than canonical.

Rank's belief in Freud's continued support is ironic, considering how he time and again criticizes Jung and towards the end of the book speaks, with evident reference to him, about "single fellow-workers" who were close to Freud but took to flight:

> *Whatever of value they found as a refuge on their ways of retreat, Freud has distinguished with remarkable objectivity from the distortions and denials of the truth only imperfectly divined; but at the same time he has eliminated*

---

[183] Otto Rank, *The Trauma of Birth* (originally published in German 1924), London 1929, p. xv.

[184] Ibid., pp. 2, 12, 106, 209, 183, 184.

them from his own field of work as not really "psychoanalytic."[185]

All this praise of Freud was to no avail. What befell Jung a dozen years earlier would with this book strike Rank. He was soon out in the cold, too.

Regardless of its deviation from Freudian doctrine, Rank's theory about the birth trauma is interesting. If there is any natural occurrence that we all share, which would have the potency of causing a trauma from early infancy and on, the moment of birth is the most likely candidate. It is a passage with the dignity only comparable to what awaits at the other end of life. Rank calls it the ultimate biological basis of the psychical.[186] We carry with us the traumatic experience of birth and long for what was before it — the comfort and peace of the mother's womb.

The longing back to the womb was also suggested by Rank's fellow disciple of Freud at the time, Sándor Ferenczi, in *Versuch einer Genitaltheorie*,[187] published the same year as Rank's book. It is referred to in Rank's text, though using a congress report from 1922.[188] Rank expresses admiration for Ferenczi's claim that "the man, penetrating into the vaginal opening, undoubtedly signifies a partial return to the womb."

Rank does not insist that the birth trauma is based on an actual memory of the event. It could just as well be what he calls a primal phantasy, "it is a matter of indifference whether the scene was experienced or not."[189]

Rank's purpose with his book is to arrange synthetically

---

[185] Ibid., p. 184.

[186] Ibid., p. xiii.

[187] It was translated to English five years after his death. Sándor Ferenczi, *Thalassa: A Theory of Genitality*, transl. Henry Alden Bunker, New York 1938.

[188] Rank, *The Trauma of Birth*, p. 39.

[189] Ibid., p. 194.

"the whole psychical development of man as shown from the analytically recognized importance of the birth trauma and in the continually recurring attempts to overcome it."[190] But he gets carried away. Rank sees the birth trauma and the longing back to the womb symbolically represented by just about everything in human culture and thought:

> *We have recognized from the analytic situation and the patient's unconscious representation of it the fundamental importance of the birth trauma, its repression and its return in neurotic reproduction, symbolic adaptation, heroic compensation, ethical reaction formation, aesthetic idealization, and philosophic speculation.*[191]

His studies of mythology have convinced him that "the human problem of birth stands actually at the centre of mythical as of infantile interest and determines conclusively the content of phantasy formations."[192] Cosmology, as it meets us not only in myths, is "nothing other than the infantile recollection of one's own birth projected on to Nature." Actually, "the whole process of culture, as reflected in myths, is only a human creation of the world on the pattern of one's own individual creation."[193]

It is not unreasonable to see the expulsion from Paradise as a symbol of the birth trauma,[194] maybe also to regard the crucifixion and resurrection of Jesus as "a repetition and reproduction of the process of birth, ethically and religiously sublimated in the sense of a neurotic overcoming of the primal

---

[190] Ibid., p. xiv.
[191] Ibid., p. 183.
[192] Ibid., p. 73.
[193] Ibid., pp. 85f.
[194] Ibid., p. 75.

trauma."[195] But explaining Nirvana, "the pleasurable Nothing," as "the womb situation" is stretching it.[196] So is his oversimplified idea of religion, hardly applicable outside Christianity and maybe Islam:

> *Every form of religion tends ultimately to the creation of a succouring and protecting primal Being to whose bosom one can flee away from all troubles and dangers and to whom one finally returns in a future life which is a faithful, although sublimated, image of the once lost Paradise.*[197]

It does not end there. Rank claims that our need for sleep is because of the birth trauma, since it makes us spend so much of our lives "in a state similar to that of the intrauterine."[198] And when we sleep, if the bedclothes slip off and we feel cold, it is "compensated for by a dream-like withdrawal into a symbolized womb."[199]

Rank also has an explanation to homosexuality: "It is based quite obviously in the case of the man on the abhorrence of the female genitals, and this because of its close relation to the shock of birth."[200] Why this abhorrence would only strike a minority of men, he neglects.

To the unconscious, any room and house symbolizes the womb,[201] whereas all implements and weapons "really directly imitate the masculine sexual organ."[202]

---

[195] Ibid., p. 137.

[196] Ibid., p. 119.

[197] Ibid., p. 117.

[198] Ibid., p. 74. Rank writes that we spend half our lives asleep, which must be some kind of typo.

[199] Ibid., p. 78.

[200] Ibid., p. 35.

[201] Ibid., pp. 86 and 88.

[202] Ibid., p. 95.

Even death itself is to the unconscious an everlasting return to the womb.[203]

Rank makes more sense, relatively speaking, when he uses his theory on astrology:

> *One might even describe astrology as the first doctrine of the birth trauma. The entire being and fate of man is determined by what occurs (in heaven) at the moment of his birth.*[204]

Applying his theory to myth and fairy tales, Rank has no trouble finding examples, some of which have already been mentioned. He explains the wooden horse used against Troy, "the only possible form of fulfilment for the Unconscious was the return into the animal-like womb."[205] The frog in the Frog-Prince fairy tale somehow represents both the penis and the fetus.[206] The setting sun is conceived "in the imagination of all races as the return of the sun to the womb (underworld),"[207] and mountains "with their hollows and caves, with their forests (hair), were looked upon as a gigantic primal mother."[208]

The hero, to whom Rank had already devoted a book, represents a type who "seeks to overcome an apparently specially severe birth trauma by a compensatory repetition of it in his deeds."[209] Only the youngest of the brothers can be the hero, since no one after him has occupied the place, in the mother.[210] Therefore, only he can return to it.

---

[203] Ibid., p. 114.
[204] Ibid., p. 117, footnote.
[205] Ibid., p. 163.
[206] Ibid., p. 111, footnote.
[207] Ibid., pp. 74f.
[208] Ibid., p. 104.
[209] Ibid., p. 107.
[210] Ibid., p. 112.

Touching on the Oedipus saga, Rank acknowledges Freud's principle of the Oedipus complex, but by introducing the man-swallowing sphinx into the equation he makes the birth trauma overrule the complex:

The Oedipus saga is certainly a duplicate of the Sphinx episode, which means psychologically that it is the repetition of the primal trauma at the sexual stage (Oedipus complex), whereas the Sphinx represents the primal trauma itself.[211]

Freud's Reaction

Freud did not take long to rebut Rank's claims. In 1926, two years after Rank's book, he published *Inhibitions, Symptoms and Anxiety*, where he dismissed Rank's birth trauma all but completely. His main argument is that it is very unlikely for anyone to have a remaining sensory impression of the time of birth.[212]

Freud also objects to the almost paradoxical elements of Rank's theory, which leave room for just about any interpretation:

Rank dwells, according as it suits him best, now on the child's recollection of its happy intra-uterine existence, now on its recollection of the traumatic disturbance which interrupted that existence; so that he is able to make almost any interpretation he pleases.[213]

Next, Freud points out anomalies, such as childhood reaction to darkness. According to Rank, it would give the comforting sense of returning to the womb, while in reality it causes anxiety in the child. Freud concludes that "the earliest phobias

---

[211] Ibid., p. 144.

[212] Sigmund Freud, *Inhibitions, Symptoms and Anxiety* (originally published in German 1926), transl. Alix Strachey, London 1936, p. 103.

[213] Ibid., p. 104.

of infancy cannot be directly traced back to impressions of birth."

Later in his book he states that his main objection to Rank's theory is that "it floats in the air instead of being based upon ascertained observations."[214] Freud is not wrong there, but the same objection can be raised about a number of his own claims, as discussed earlier in this book.

Death, Though
Freud's major objection, about the birth not being memorable, is probable but not ascertained, as he himself admits. Rank, though, implies even more. Since his theory is based on not just the birth trauma but also the longing for a return to the mother's womb, it suggests some kind of memory of the time before birth. Without a pleasant memory of the existence in the womb, we can't long for a return to it.

It was not scientifically confirmed at the time of Rank's and Freud's books, but there are things the fetus perceives, especially at the time approaching birth. Its hearing is particularly developed, even to the point that it can recognize words and differentiate between voices.[215] So, the basic condition for Rank's theory has actually been confirmed. But his idea of a birth trauma is still in need of confirmation, and his far-fetched applications of it are easily disproved.

Although we might have at least fragments of memories from our birth, even from the time preceding it, the question is if that would create a longing back to the womb. I dare say that the thought is absurd, if not revolting, to just about all of us. It would be like not wanting to live at all. In order to claim that a traumatic wish of that kind is strong in us all, Rank would have needed to present mightily convincing arguments. He did not.

Reading his book, it is hard to escape the impression that

---

[214] Ibid., p. 134.

[215] Ferris Jabr, "Study of Fetal Perception Takes Off," *Scientific American* (scientificamerican.com), 2015.

he was seduced by the simplicity and strong symbolism of his idea of the birth trauma. He wanted to make his theory as big as he felt it was good. And deep. Being a psychoanalyst, he also had to make it fit that paradigm, with its concept of neurosis and human frustration as the yoke we all carry. Add to that the presumed secret workings of the unconscious.

Of course, birth is a major event in our lives. The significance of our very first breath is only equaled by our last. So, there is no mystery in the symbol of it showing up in so much of what we think and do. That does not necessarily mean we have a traumatic relation to it. It happened and we survived it. We move on.

Rank would probably have made a better case for a fundamental trauma if he created it around our knowledge of our mortality. We all know that we will die, and there is no escaping it.

There are certainly many ingredients in myths and religious doctrines referring to birth, but so many more, with so much more amplitude, regarding death. We don't have to relive our birth in order to overcome it, but we do through life feel an increasing need to come to peace with the certainty of our approaching death. Some religions even have a comforting promise about that as their main attraction.

Looking at mythologies, it is certainly evident that they usually speculate about the birth of humankind as well as that of the whole world. The overwhelming majority of deities were also once born, but the big thing about most of them is that contrary to men they do not die. That is the decisive trait setting them apart from humans. Some deities, such as Yahweh, have not even been born but were around forever. Still, their lack of birth matters little, since they exist. The thing is that they will continue to exist forever.

It is clearly pointed out in the religious source most familiar to Freud and all his disciples, which is the Bible. When Yahweh finds that Adam and Eve have eaten the forbidden fruit, he hurries to expel them from the garden so that they do not get to eat of the fruit that will make them immortal. It would make them his equals.[216] And Christianity is built on the idea that Jesus died for our sins, though he was not dead for more than a couple of days. After that, being divine, he does not die anymore.

It is all about death, and not birth. Each of the four Gospels portrays the death of Jesus in detail, but only two of them speak of his birth (and childhood) at all.[217] Even the expression "born-again Christian" is meaningful because of the promise that it leads to eternal life beyond the moment of death. Without this feature, the rebirth would be a short-lived solace.

The scarce psychoanalytical focus on death causing frustration is surprising. It may stem from the fact that there is no analytical method to avoid it, probably not even to come to terms with it. It is a quest on which each of us is fundamentally alone, where a therapist has little to contribute.

The Double

But Rank did write a book where death and the fear of it are discussed: *The Double*, first published in 1914, revised and expanded in 1925, the year after *The Trauma of Birth* was originally released. In this book he traces the concept of a double, as in a shadow or soul or guardian angel, through superstitious beliefs, myths, and fiction.

He sees this phenomenon as a narcissistic expression, one that reached obsessive proportion in several of our great authors. E. T. A. Hoffmann, Edgar Allan Poe, Guy de Maupassant, and Fyodor Dostoyevsky are among the ones examined.

The fascination with this double can become a fixation, and ultimately lead to death. Rank lists plenty of old superstitions and legends from many cultures, which warn about the danger of seeing one's double, be it in a vision or in a mirror

---

[216] Genesis 3:22.

[217] The Gospels of Matthew and Luke. Mark and John commence with the baptism of Jesus as an adult.

— like the tragic fate of Narcissus caught by his reflection in the water. The double is a dangerous acquaintance. Rank quotes E. T. A. Hoffmann:

It is the phantom of our own Self, whose intimate relationship with, and deep effect upon, our spirit casts us into hell or transports us into Heaven.[218]

To Rank, the double is in essence the narcissistic adoration of oneself and none other. Of course, the greatest threat to the narcissist is erasure of the self, as in death. It is not that death as such is feared, but the idea that it will erase the self, which can become so unbearable to the narcissist that he paradoxically commits or at least considers suicide to end the torment:

Thus we have the strange paradox of the suicide who voluntarily seeks death in order to free himself of the intolerable thanatophobia.[219]

The only salvation would be if somehow the self could survive death. This is precisely what many conceptions of the double imply, be it the shadow or the soul or something similar. Death takes one of the two, but not both. The narcissist's self lives on in the double.

It is implied by Rank's reasoning that we all have at least a fragment of that narcissistic urge for self-preservation also into the beyond, and he sees it expressed loud and clear in society:

The primitive belief in souls is originally nothing else than a kind of belief in immortality which energetically denies

---

[218] Otto Rank, *The Double: A Psychoanalytic Study* (*Der Doppelgänger: Eine Psychoanalytische Studie*, 1925), transl. Harry Tucker jr., New York 1979, p. 69.

[219] Ibid., p. 78.

> *the power of death; and even today the essential content of the belief in the soul — as it subsists in religion, superstition, and modern cults — has not become other, nor much more, than that. The thought of death is rendered supportable by assuring oneself of a second life, after this one, as a double.*[220]

Rank exaggerates when he insists that making this so-called narcissistic wish to preserve one's self is pathological. It can become so, when leading to neurotic behavior and even suicide. Basically, though, it is not only natural but essential for us to foster a fascination with what we are and what is inside of us as individuals, or we would be no more than lumps of meat. Like Oblomov, in Ivan Goncharov's 1859 novel with the same name, we would not even leave our beds.

Through human history, there have been many beliefs in the ever after, and almost as many proposed reasons for them, psychological or in other terminologies. Rank points to the need itself and how it is expressed. It is indeed worth pondering, since this need evidently sidetracks reason and frequently makes people reject even the basic instinct of bodily survival.

The deep urge to preserve the self eternally gives clues to how we perceive ourselves — unique and irreplaceable. It also hints at what we need to make our lives meaningful, as well as why we need to do so. Surely, some of the finest human accomplishments in history — and some of the worst — have been nourished by this need.

The idea of a double is not far-fetched, nor is an intensified or even hallucinatory impression of one. Rank mentions the actual shadow that light makes appear beside us as one phenomenon stimulating the belief in a double. But it is doubtful that even primeval man would take very long figuring out the cause of the shadow and how it operates. Furthermore, primeval man could see it formed beside even inanimate objects.

---

[220] Ibid., pp. 84f.

Fantasies about that physical shadow are more likely to have been amusements, or symbols not meant to be taken literally.

What is much more relevant to the idea of the double is the fact that we are able not only to separate ourselves from everything and everyone in our surroundings, but also to reflect upon ourselves and our actions as if being our own audience — and critic, as the psychoanalysts have told us in so many words. As we live our lives, we continuously observe and contemplate ourselves. That is indeed a double.

Another one is the self in our dreams. It is not the same one as the person walking around when we are awake, since that one lies still. The mystery of our dreams must be one of the most influential phenomena in creating all kinds of beliefs and conceptions of an immaterial reality. It is another double, and the most puzzling one. Primeval man must have wondered if that self died when the awake self did. At least it was open to speculation, since the truth of the matter was impossible to ascertain.

With this book of his, Rank touches on several perspectives of great interest to the study of the human condition. It is significant that he does so with much less of the psychoanalytical terminology and apparatus, than in his books previously discussed. He finds more use for concepts borrowed from art and poetry, from mythical concepts themselves rather than psychoanalytical translations of them. That speaks to his advantage.

Otto Rank's thoughts about the double as well as those about the birth trauma are interesting, and his ability to target such essential concepts of the human psyche was impressive. Who knows what they would have led him to, if he were not so tied up by Freud's doctrine, even when dismissed by his teacher? Sadly, he died so soon after Freud did, there was no time for him to explore the freedom it must have given his mind.

Franz Riklin

Franz Riklin (1878-1938) was a Swiss psychiatrist who joined the psychoanalytical movement already in the first decade of the 20th century, famously working with Carl G. Jung on their word association test, leading to a joint treatise in 1904.[221] When Jung broke with Freud, Riklin stayed by Freud's side, but ceased to practice psychoanalysis.

His son with the same name, on the other hand, was analyzed by Jung and joined his movement to remain active with it all his life.

His father's contributions were not that noticed, except for the experiments he did with Jung, but while still in the Freudian sphere he wrote a study on fairy tales discussed below. It was published already in 1908 and follows Freud's doctrine rather slavishly, expressing great praise for him. It was at a time when also Jung was still a faithful pupil of Freud. The English translation of the book appeared in 1915.

Sex in Fairy Tales

Riklin goes through a number of fairy tales to extract their sexual symbolism and patterns conforming to the Oedipus complex. He finds it surprising how great a role the sexual plays in fairy tales,[222] but that can come as no surprise since he selects fairy tales of the girl-meets-prince or boy-meets-princess kind. Not that they are hard to find. These stories speak about love and living happily ever after, but of course there is sexual innuendo to be found in them.

---

[221] C. G. Jung & Fr. Riklin, "Experimentelle Untersuchungen über Assoziationen Gesunder", *Journal für Psychologie und Neurologie*, Band III, Heft 5, 1904, pp. 193-215.

[222] Franz Riklin (spelled Ricklin in this edition), *Wishfulfillment and Symbolism in Fairy Tales* (*Wunscherfüllung und Symbolik im Märchen*, 1908), transl. Wm. A. White, New York 1915, p. 3.

Riklin sees it just about everywhere, thanks to his generous assigning of sexual symbols, some more obvious than others. The serpent is not far-fetched as a symbol of the male organ, though Riklin admits that not every fairy tale serpent is a sexual symbol.[223] Also, the frog might be a symbol of fertilization in some stories, such as when transformed to a prince by being kissed on the lips.[224] At that event it may also be reasonable to see the woman's mouth as a symbol of her sexual organ.[225]

Less convincing is a dream analysis where the long street is a passage in the female genitals.[226] Questionable is also the statement that dragons, serpents, giants, devils, and monsters commonly play the same role, by which he means the sexual innuendo.[227]

The sexual symbols Riklin sees are to him evidence of infantile sexual theories, which have led to the view that "this masking of sexual processes took its origin in the telling of fairy stories by women."[228] It is unclear if he shares this peculiar view.

As for the presence of the Oedipus complex in those fairy tales, it is a matter of interpretation, and Riklin is of course quite biased in his.

Franz Riklin is included here because of his presence in the early group around Freud and Jung, but also because his text discusses fairy tales as highly comparable to myths:

Some render, apparently unaltered, old myths, which we analyze with success as psychological wholes. Others con-

---

[223] Ibid., p. 37.

[224] Ibid., p. 39.

[225] Ibid., p. 51.

[226] Ibid., p. 29.

[227] Ibid., p. 36.

[228] Ibid., p. 61.

> *tain and utilize only fragments of myths as material for a new one that again is complete in itself.*[229]

This is because they have a common denominator and origin in dreams of wish-fulfillment. He admits that they have somewhat separate causes and functions, but as for fairy tales he is quite certain of their link to the psyche of Freud's design: "For the psychology of fairy tales, as we have learned to know through Freud, stands in close relationship to the world of dreams, of hysteria, and of mental disease."[230] Their symbolism, "chiefly constructed from the unconscious," is also found in dreams and psychopathology.

Fairy tales bring two sets of symbols from different sources together:

> *Here two symbolic series unite and often overlap; one develops from the aspects of magic, mythology, and religion, the other is the symbolism of dreams and of psychopathology. It is true they originate from the same spring, the human psyche.*[231]

The last sentence is superfluous. Where else could they come from but the human psyche? He goes on to explain that although fairy tales share many of their symbols with mythology, the construction of the latter is different. First and foremost, they come from personification:

> *The forces that influence mankind are personified, natural phenomena and inexplicable inner experiences (dreams, nightmare). In place of the real, active forces, anthropomorphic beings are substituted.*

---

[229] Ibid., p. 1.

[230] Ibid.

[231] Ibid., p. 27.

This view on the origin of myths is shared by a long line of commentators since the days of Ancient Greece.

Riklin mainly compares the content of fairy tales to the wish dreams of which Freud spoke in his *The Interpretation of Dreams*, and explains how a fairy tale is born:

> *The poet, whose longings reality can not still, creates for himself, quite unconsciously, in phantasy, what life has denied to him.*[232]

Riklin points out that there are many fairy tales in which the poor peasant maid marries a prince and the shepherd boy a princess, exclaiming triumphantly: "Those are wish structures!"[233] Well, nobody is arguing that. A lot of entertainment from the past as well as the present is. However, that is no proof of the wishes being oedipal.

He gives examples of fairy tales with evil step-mothers and incestuous kingly fathers, both usually meeting a well-deserved end. These stories may certainly share a few traits with that of King Oedipus, but also significant differences. The fairy tale heroes are reluctant, revolting, and escaping. That speaks not of some unconscious urge to kill one parent in order to mate the other, but simply of self-defense.

The plot pattern of the kind of fairy tales Riklin utilizes is quite plain and obvious: A pleasant situation is interrupted by threats and ordeals, which are finally overcome to reach an even pleasanter situation. Things get worse before they get better. All's well that ends well.

That Is Any Story

Any story shows much of the same structure or it would fail to attract an audience. A situation going from good to better to best might be wishful thinking, but as a story it is just boring.

---

[232] Ibid., p. 5.

[233] Ibid., p. 14.

One going from bad to worse is neither appealing nor that much less boring. The only working order is from bad to good, or from good to bad to very good.

What Riklin sees as signs of the inner workings of the unconscious, are narrative necessities to make a story exciting. He is far from alone among the psychoanalysts to ignore this.

There is also the type of story called tragedy, which was favored by Aristotle as well as many playwrights. It goes from good to bad, ending with catastrophe. It may seem strange that such dramas belong to the most popular ones in the history of theater and literature, although they can hardly be seen as any kind of wishful thinking. Aristotle explained it as catharsis, the emotional release it brought the audience.

Tragic endings are rare in fairy tales, but they do exist. They often display a harsh moral — the hero fails utterly and therefore meets a bitter end. Mythology is full of them, usually with the pattern of the Orpheus and Eurydice myth: When bringing his love back from the realm of the dead, Orpheus could not resist looking back at Eurydice on the way, thereby losing her forever. In the Bible, Lot's wife met a similar fate, turning into a pillar of salt as she looked back when fleeing Sodom.[234]

Although such fairy tales are rare to find among all the ones with happy endings, they present something of an anomaly to Riklin's wish-fulfillment principle. But a great number of fairy tales definitely conform to it — also those that end happily without any wedlock or love affair at all.

This should have told Riklin that though the wish-fulfillment is very common in fairy tales, it rarely includes something fitting the Oedipus complex, in spite of his tendentious selection of stories.

---

[234] Genesis 19:26.

Ernest Jones

The Welsh psychoanalyst Ernest Jones (1879-1958) befriended Freud in 1908 and they remained on friendly terms even through some controversies. Jones was also the one recommending Freud to form the so-called Secret Society of those committed to his doctrine, and deeply involved in the behind-the-scenes activities of Freud's core followers competing to prove their loyalty to him.[235]

Apart from *The Life and Work of Sigmund Freud* in three volumes, published between 1953 and 1957, Jones's writing on psychoanalysis was neither as voluminous nor as significant as that of some of his colleagues. But he did write some essays about psychoanalytical perspectives on certain themes in folklore, mythology, and superstition.

Also, he analyzed *Hamlet* as an expression of the Oedipus complex. His initial text on this subject was from 1910, with expanded revisions in 1911 and 1949.

Spilling Salt

In his 1912 essay "The Symbolic Significance of Salt in Folklore and Superstition," Ernest Jones made a psychoanalytical examination of the old superstition that it brings bad luck to spill salt. In spite of the seemingly marginal subject, his text spans almost a hundred pages, where he goes through a great number of beliefs, folklore fragments, and rituals surrounding the real or imagined potency of salt and its significance in human culture.

He concludes from all of this that "the idea of salt has derived much of its significance from its being unconsciously associated with that of semen."[236]

---

[235] See Grosskurth, *The Secret Ring*, 1991.

[236] Ernest Jones, "The Symbolic Significance of Salt in Folklore and Super-

Oddly, he is not very clear on how that would lead to the superstition about spilling salt, but it is implied that it could have to do with premature ejaculation: "It acts, in other words, by disturbing the harmony of two people previously engaged in amicable intercourse."[237] Therefore:

> *The idea of salt in folk-lore and superstition characteristically represents the male, active, fertilising principle.*[238]

As Jones states in his text, there is no mystery to the symbolic significance of salt. The precious substance has the ability to conserve food, and the strange property of those rock-hard crystals to dissolve quickly in water, among other things. But an unconscious connection of it to semen is far-fetched. Already their different states of matter, one being solid and the other liquid, speak against it. Still, Jones states that the symbols we pick should be the most obvious ones:

> *There appears to be a general tendency of the human mind to symbolise objects and interests of paramount and universal significance in forms that are psychologically the most suitable and available.*[239]

What is obvious to him is obviously not so to everyone else. Although also doubtful, Jones's claim that alcohol is another unconscious symbol for semen[240] makes more sense. At least, it is liquid and its effect on the psyche is much more intricate than that of salt.

Ancient beliefs have linked semen to the other bodily flu-

---

stition" (originally published in *Imago* 1912), *Essays in Applied Psycho-Analysis*, London 1923, p. 135.

[237] Ibid., p. 196.

[238] Ibid., p. 199.

[239] Ibid., p. 201.

[240] Ibid., p. 139.

ids, though they were always understood to have different functions.

The superstition regarding spilling salt finds a much easier explanation in the fact that in the past it was precious and in many parts of the world difficult to come by. Having it was fortunate and losing it unfortunate. Mystery solved.

Jones also touches on the custom of reversing the bad luck by throwing salt over one's shoulder as a counter-charm, but he admits to not exploring that aspect fully:

> *The explanation of why the salt has to be thrown* backwards, *and why precisely over the* left *shoulder, would open up themes too extensive for us to enter on here; it is one of the many respects in which the analysis offered in this essay remains incomplete.*[241]

Well, isn't the backwards throw for a psychoanalyst the obvious measure to invoke a reversion? Otherwise, it would just be spilling more salt. The left shoulder can be explained by the fact that most people are right-handed and therefore they more conveniently throw the salt to the left.

There is another thing with superstitions, which tends to be ignored by the psychoanalysts. By time, many superstitious activities become customs, even when people have since long stopped believing in them. Instead of being thought of as charms or counter-charms, they have simply become little rituals done for no other reason than that they conform to the ways of old. There is comfort in that, and much can be said about our need to link to the habits of our predecessors. It is a significant part of our cultural behavior and our reason for it. But it is irrelevant to treat it as superstition.

This is shown in our relation to salt. In modern society it is easily accessible in quantity, consequently old symbolic and magical values formerly assigned to it fade away. Some of the

---

[241] Ibid., p. 198.

customs regarding salt remain, though depraved of their urgency and importance. They are nowadays mere amusements.

That in turn raises the question if superstitions were ever firm convictions, or just shared figments of imagination, elements of "what if" more than beliefs.

A Dove in the Ear

In 1914, two years after the previous essay, Ernest Jones published a text with similar theme and approach: *The Madonna's Conception through the Ear*. This time he examined psychoanalytical aspects of the peculiarities of the Annunciation, especially — as stated by some medieval church fathers and shown in some medieval art — the Madonna's impregnation through the ear.

He quotes what he mistakenly believes to be written by Augustine: "Deus per angelum loquebatur et Virgo per aurem impraegnebatur" ("God spoke through the angel and the Virgin was impregnated by ear").[242] Among the art works mentioned are Annunciation paintings by Filippo Lippi, Benozzo Gozzoli, and Simone Martini. The painting by Martini is discussed in detail and reproduced on the frontispiece of the 1923 book.

Jones's choice of mythological subjects is quite particular. In this case, it gives the impression that there is also a sense of humor involved. He examines the depicting of how Mary got impregnated with Jesus through the ear, by the agents of the archangel Gabriel and a dove. The latter was, of course, the classical representation of the Holy Spirit. So, the conception was done by God's breath. Jones, though, has a take on it that deviates radically from the Christian view.

Coming to his own conclusions, he has the same method

---

[242] Ernest Jones, "The Madonna's Conception through the Ear: A Contribution to the Relation between Aesthetics and Religion" (originally published in *Jahrbuch der Psychoanalyse* 1914), *Essays in Applied Psycho-Analysis*, London 1923, p. 264. The quote is from *Sermones de Tempore*, falsely attributed to Augustine.

as with the previous essay — a lengthy list of examples from mythology, superstitions, and art history selected to support his case. The quantity of examples has little weight, since it is evident cherry picking all through. From the multitude of myths and artistic objects, he only chooses those in support of his theory and does not investigate even one that lacks this support or contradicts it. As evidence it is of no value.

Also, he insists on the Freudian idea that unconscious impressions and beliefs are formed in early childhood and therefore based on its misconceptions of sexuality and bodily functions. That, too, is in dire need of confirmation. He has none other than that it has been stated by Freud and his disciples in writing, and supposedly supported by experiences from therapy work.

His conclusions, from this dubious research, are spectacular to the point of absurd. He claims that the wind of God's breath really refers to the breaking of wind humans do from their anal orifice, the white dove is a phallus, and Maria's ear is a symbol of her anus. The reason for all of this is that these things represent ignorant childish beliefs about human reproduction, stuck in the unconscious all through adulthood. In other words, it is based on the ABC of Freudian doctrine. He states:

> *It is a law of psychogenesis, founded now on extensive experience, that an idea can become psychically important in adult life only through becoming associated with, and reinforcing, an earlier chain of ideas reaching back into childhood, and that much, or even most, of its psychical (as apart from intrinsic) significance is derived from these.*[243]

That claim demands a number of elaborate arguments and the negligence of explanations closer at hand. About the ear representing the anus instead of the vagina, Jones explains

[243] Ibid., p. 272.

that the child knows nothing of the existence of the vagina,[244] which is yet another indication of Freudian doctrine focusing on the perspectives of the male gender. The Freudian importance given to the anus is also shown when he continues with this rather drastic statement:

> *Such habits as nose and ear-picking, for instance, invariably prove on analysis to be derivatives of, and substitutes for, anal masturbation.*

About the creative wind, Jones points out that the breath from the mouth lacks both the sound and the odor of its lower counterpart, which is what triggers infants. Thus, "the acts of breathing and speaking are both treated in the Unconscious as equivalents of the act of passing intestinal flatus."[245]

But while the latter is occasional and of minor importance, the upper breath is both constant and so vital that it is impossible to persevere for more than a few minutes without it. Jones admits to breath as a symbol of life and the presence or absence of it is the simplest and most primitive test of death.[246] Indeed, it is the foremost expression of being alive and staying alive. Even a child can get that. Furthermore, any child is able to produce a much louder sound from its mouth than from its anus, already in its infancy.

The white dove as a symbol of the Holy Spirit is equally evident without any reference to sexual organs. It flies through the air, its color is that of purity, like the clouds in heaven that carry no threats, and it is regarded as a messenger since the time of Noah.

As for the tradition of conception through the ear, it was necessary to be another bodily orifice than the usual one, since Mary was in Christian dogma firmly stated to be a virgin also

---

[244] Ibid., p. 342.
[245] Ibid., p. 289.
[246] Ibid., p. 270.

after this act. Moreover, Mary is informed of her pregnancy by the words of Gabriel, just as God had performed the whole world creation by words. She is impregnated by hearing God's command.

It is clearly indicated by the Simone Martini Annunciation painting used as a frontispiece to Jones's book. There, the words from Gabriel's mouth are written on a line right at Mary's ear.

There is a general objection to be made against the Freudian claim of childish misconceptions taking form in the unconscious, which is also Jones's claim. He shows in his text reasons for these misconceptions that are, however faulty, results of logical assumptions. Children make conclusions from observations, which must be a conscious process also by psychoanalytical standards. Children are aware of them and would therefore be continuously aware of facts learned later, correcting their previous errors.

That contradicts the idea of a petrified unconscious influence unbeknownst to the growing child even into adulthood.

On a sidenote, in this text from 1914 Jones makes use of the term archetype, which is five years before Jung would do the same in his writing. It is just once, when describing incest as "the great archetype" of sin.[247]

Effeminate God

Ernest Jones returned to the subject of Mary's conception by the ear in a lecture given at a psychoanalytical congress in 1922: *A Psycho-Analytic Study of the Holy Ghost*. He repeats his claims about the nature of God's creative breath and Mary's ear, but then he goes on with additional interpretations of the Holy Ghost and its implications, none less radical than his previous views.

Jones states that Christianity has replaced an original trinity of the father, the mother, and the son with one that excludes

[247] Ibid., p. 302.

the mother to insert the Holy Ghost, which emanates from the father. To no surprise, he finds the reason for it in the Oedipus complex:

> *The replacement of the Mother-Goddess by the Holy Ghost is a manifestation of the desirability of renouncing incestuous and parricidal wishes and replacing them by a stronger attachment to the Father.*[248]

By excluding the mother from the trinity, the father inherits to some extent the motherly qualities, as indicated in Christianity by the submissive love devoted to their god and the love the god has for them. Even the dove by which Mary gets impregnated is "one of the most effeminate of all the phallic emblems."

A milder deity replaces the stern and fearsome father of the Old Testament. Furthermore, "the opportunity is given of winning the Father's love by the adoption of a feminine attitude towards him."[249]

This leads to something of a homosexual cult, "the extensive part played by sublimated homosexuality throughout the Christian religion,"[250] as seen by the importance of brotherly love, monks denying their male traits in what Jones describes as a symbolic self-castration, as well as in the celibacy of Catholic priests and the fanciful attire with which they dress themselves.

But the worship of the mother was partly reinstated, since "the human need for a Mother to worship was too strong." Mariolatry emerged, leading to the papal decree that she herself was also conceived immaculately. Still, this reinstatement of the mother did not change the homosexual attitude in reli-

---

[248] Ernest Jones, "A Psycho-Analytic Study of the Holy Ghost" (1922), *Essays in Applied Psycho-Analysis*, London 1923, p. 425.

[249] Ibid., pp. 422f.

[250] Ibid., p. 425.

gion. Instead, "all the self-castrating tendencies are more evident where Mariolatry is highly developed."[251]

Protestantism, on the other hand, seeks to regain the male characteristics, by allowing priests to marry, cleaning their attire as well as the churches from exaggerated decorations, and so on. They succeed in this by resisting the Catholic tendency of Mariolatry. Jones ends his lecture:

> *One might perhaps say that the Protestant solution of the Oedipus complex is the replacement of the Mother by the Woman, while the Catholic one consists in the change of the masculine to the feminine attitude.*

Where to begin? Looking at the Annunciation, there is nothing "effeminate" about a male god impregnating a woman, nor is it anything new in the world of mythology. The extraordinary measures by which this is accomplished with Mary can be explained by the need to keep her a virgin all through, as discussed above. So, it would be at least as plausible that the exclusion of the mother from the trinity makes the god and the religion renounce femininity instead of embracing it.

As for Jones's theories about homosexuality, they might be excused by the prejudice of the time in which his text was written, were it not for their prominence also in the texts of other Freudians, including those of their mentor. The doctrine of psychoanalysis was not only persistently prejudiced against women, but also in its treatment of homosexuality — to the point where it would not be completely irrelevant to apply the modern term homophobia.[252]

---

[251] Ibid., pp. 429f.

[252] The term *homophobia* was introduced by the American psychologist George Weinberg in the 1960's.

Oskar Pfister

Oskar Pfister (1873-1956) was a Swiss priest and teacher who worked to incorporate psychoanalysis and its perspective into the religious context. He also applied it to education. Together with Eugen Bleuler in Zurich, he founded the Swiss Society for Psychoanalysis, which was dissolved in 1914 when Carl G. Jung and others turned away from the Freudian doctrine. Together with Emil Oberholzer, he founded the society anew in 1919.[253]

In 1908, Pfister visited Sigmund Freud for the first time. They had an ongoing correspondence until 1937, two years before Freud's death. Many of those letters were published in the volume *Psychoanalysis and Faith*, 1963. As the title emphasizes, the subject in the letters was often, but not exclusively, religion. The atheist and the pastor certainly had their disagreements on this issue, but they remained close friends and Pfister stayed a supporter of Freud's theory of psychoanalysis all through.[254]

Pfister had problems being accepted by some other psychoanalysts, though, since he had no formal medical education. This was regarded as a prerequisite — also initially by Freud, but he grew to change his mind. In the introduction to Pfister's book *The Psychoanalytic Method* from 1913, Freud wrote:

> *It may be asked whether the practice of psychoanalysis does not presuppose a medical education which must remain lacking to the educator and pastor, or whether other relations are not antagonistic to the purpose of placing the psychoanalytic technique in other than medical hands. I con-*

---

[253] Alexander et al., 1966, p.170.

[254] Heinrich Meng & Ernst L. Freud (ed.), *Psychoanalysis and Faith. The Letters of Sigmund Freud and Oskar Pfister*, transl. Eric Mosbacher, New York 1963, pp. 7 and 9.

fess that I see no such obstacles. The practice of psychoanalysis demands much less medical education than psychological preparation and free human insight; the majority of physicians, however, are not fitted for the practice of psychoanalysis and have completely failed in placing a correct valuation on this method of treatment.[255]

Psychoanalysis for Missionaries

In 1921, Oskar Pfister wrote an article for a German journal on missiology and religious studies (*Zeitschrift für Missionskunde und Religionswissenschaft*) on how to apply psychoanalysis in missionary work. The English translation of it was two years later included in his book *Some Applications of Psycho-Analysis*.

At that time, psychoanalysis was still new, and far from generally accepted as a science, whereas missionaries had been active around the world for centuries, which led Pfister to ask this rhetorical question:

Must mission work, in spite of its reverend age, sit at the feet of a science that is no older than yesterday?[256]

He finds that the psychology of religion had been "hardly fruitful" for the missionary, but it was "fertilized" by the introduction of psychoanalysis. It gives the tools for understanding the religious process, comparable to what X-rays and other examinations bring to medicine.

He continues by describing what it can uncover about religion:

The aim of psycho-analysis as applied to religion is the research into the subliminal motives of pious consciousness

---

[255] Oskar Pfister, *The Psychoanalytic Method*, transl. Charles Rockwell Payne, New York 1917 (originally published in German 1913), p. vii.

[256] Oskar Pfister, *Some Applications of Psycho-Analysis*, unnamed translator, London 1923 (originally published in German 1920 and 1921), p. 316.

and its effects, as well as its causal derivation and biological knowledge.[257]

He is very confident about the curing power of psychoanalysis:

I have seen hundreds of mistaken people wandering in the paths of evil and religious perversity who had been treated by the traditional methods without success, but were saved (sometimes easily, and sometimes only with great difficulty) by psycho-analytical treatment.[258]

The mistake and perversity are those of not having the true Christian faith. The truth is revealed to them: "Analysis helps us to grasp what is false and to destroy illusions." Accordingly, it can only be used to reach a Christian experience and conviction, since it is to Pfister the only truth. He regards other religions as neurotic and even calls Jesus the first psychoanalyst.[259] Other religions don't stand a chance:

The Buddhist missionary cannot apply psycho-analysis because it would lay bare the pathological nature of his own religion.

Harsh words. His pick of Buddhism as an example is unfortunate, since it can be discussed if it strictly speaking is a religion, in the sense of worshipping a deity and other attributes Christians normally associate with it. The Buddhist process of self-cultivation might more accurately be described as a form of therapy.

Pfister's idea about the truth revealed by psychoanalysis is not only limited to Christianity, but to the form of it that is

[257] Ibid., p. 319.
[258] Ibid., p. 321.
[259] Ibid., p. 328.

his: "Protestant religion, which is free from neurosis."[260] Furthermore, it should be void of the pomp of dogma, and focus on what he regards as its essence: "The spirit of love is everything."[261] He grieves how modern society has corrupted Christianity:

> *We have no right to imagine that our European Christianity is pure and authentic! We have made such a hateful pact between our Christianity and Mars and Mammon, between the spirit of caste and national self-esteem, between lying politics and expansion, that a pure evangelical mission is a bitter necessity for our churches and our hearts.*

Psychoanalysis must be a tremendous tool to navigate through all those obstacles and reach salvation.

Neurotic Religion
Oskar Pfister's firm conviction of his own religion as the only true one, and the ultimate result of psychoanalysis, makes him a flawed theorist on the psychological causes and mechanisms of religion. That cannot be done when excluding his own religion from the study. Still, that is what he does, without even arguing for this omission.

He bases his theories on what he calls natural religions, by which he means primitive ones, and regards them as having originated in magic as a method against anxiety, which he separates from fear: "Fear appears only when there is real danger; anxiety without it." It is the fear of the unknown.[262]

The theory of religion born out of magic was widespread at his time, explained as a will to control what was really uncontrollable. Anxiety was certainly part of it, but of course there was real danger involved. Life among so-called primi-

---

[260] Ibid., p. 336.
[261] Ibid., pp. 342f.
[262] Ibid., p. 330.

tives was not safe. People had many reasons to be scared, and tried magic against both known and unknown threats.

As Pfister mentions, magic was also used in efforts to gain things, not just as protection.[263] That has nothing to do with the anxiety of which he speaks. What he adds to the mix is that by time, this behavior became neurotic: "magic and obsessional neurotic rituals are one and the same." He concludes, stressing it with italics:

> *Obsessional neurosis is private magic; the magic of primitive peoples is a collective obsessional neurosis.*

Not only is it lacking as an explanation to the origin of religion, but to the extent that it is valid it goes for Christianity as well. This religion, too, contains methods by which to control the uncontrollable, even beyond the moment of death. Prayer is a magic spell and the worship of a higher power is a measure by which to gain its benevolence.

But that is far from everything religion encompasses, neither Christianity nor any other one. Religions have many functions, which they all more or less share. Pfister is well aware of the complexity of his own faith, but presents nothing that fundamentally separates it from other religions, except his claim that it is the one that is true. He has the burden of proof on that statement, but never presents it. To him, that is just how it is.

An amusing example of his bias is found in what he calls the fixation to the father and its influence on religious worship. But what Jesus "in His capacity of profound psychologist" presented as an antidote was God in that role: "God as Father is the greatest help in the fight against the father as god."[264]

That may be a different father, somehow, but it increases instead of lessens the father fixation. This is at the core of Freud's idea about how religion emerged: God was an image

---

[263] Ibid., p. 331.
[264] Ibid., pp. 344f.

of the father, a product of the Oedipus complex. Pfister would have benefited from instead focusing on how Jesus transformed the image of that supreme deity from a stern and punishing father into a loving one.

The Illusion of a Future of an Illusion

In 1927, Sigmund Freud's *The Future of an Illusion*, discussed earlier, was released. To a significant extent, the book was the result of his correspondence with Oskar Pfister on the subject of religion.

In a letter to him a few weeks before the book was to be published, Freud expressed his hesitation about the book, as well as his respect for Pfister:

> *I had been wanting to write it for a long time, and postponed it out of regard for you, but the impulse became too strong. The subject-matter — as you will easily guess — is my completely negative attitude to religion, in any form and however attenuated, and, though there can be nothing new to you in this, I feared, and still fear, that such a public profession of my attitude will be painful to you. When you have read it you must let me know what measure of toleration and understanding you are able to preserve for the hopeless pagan.*[265]

He even encouraged Pfister to publish his objections to the book, which was done in Freud's journal *Imago* the following year.[266]

In opposition to Freud's dismissal of religion, Pfister in-

---

[265] Meng & Freud (ed.) 1963, pp. 109f.

[266] Oskar Pfister, "The Illusion of a Future: A Friendly Disagreement with Prof. Sigmund Freud," transl. Susan Abrams & Tom Taylor, ed. Paul Roazen, *The International Journal of Psycho-Analysis*, vol. 74 issue 3, London 1993 (originally published in German in *Imago*, vol. XIV, 1928), pp. 559 and 557.

sists on its values — at least when it comes to Protestant Christianity, as it has developed, which is the one of his own conviction. He recognizes the element of neurotic compulsion in religion of which Freud speaks, but mainly in the primitive forms of it, lacking the structure of a church:

> *These compulsions are unmistakeable in many primitive religions, which as yet have nothing of a proper ecclesiastical structure as in the various orthodoxies.*[267]

With Jesus, Pfister states, religion evolved from this flawed original form, and here he repeats his comparison of Jesus to a psychoanalyst:

> *Jesus overcame the collective neurosis of his people according to good psychoanalytical practice in that he introduced love — morally complete love, to be sure — into the centre of life.*[268]

The extent to which he connects Jesus with psychoanalysis is baffling, calling his practice of it subtle, with the only reservation that it should not rob Freud of being the pioneer of the discipline:

> *Not that one should put Jesus forward as the first psychoanalyst in Freud's sense, as some saucy young know-it-alls would perhaps like to do! But his redemptive ministry, in its basic traits, so decisively points in the direction of analysis that Christians should be ashamed to have left it to a non-Christian to make use of these radiant footprints.*[269]

The teaching of Jesus changed the image of God, so that

---

[267] Ibid., p. 560.
[268] Ibid., p. 561.
[269] Ibid., p. 562.

"God had to appear as loving and no longer as the strict, jealous God of the Old Testament."[270]

There is no end to what good comes out of religion, according to Pfister, and he finds it mostly in Protestant Christianity. For the long listing below, he claims that these feelings are inaccessible to irreligious persons, and it is a lot of which they are deprived:

> *Religion concerns itself with the question of the meaning and value of life; with the unifying drive of the intellect toward a universal view that encompasses existence and obligation; with the longing for home and peace; with the drive toward a* unio mystica *with the absolute; with the spiritual bonds of guilt and with freedom's thirst for grace; with the need for a love that is removed from the unbearable insecurity of earthly life; with innumerable other matters that, in their resettled state, distress and choke the soul, yet through religious counterbalancing lift up human life to radiant mountain peaks with views into the distance that make one indescribably happy, strengthen the heart, and, through the imposition of very heavy moral obligations in the spirit of love, enhance the value of existence.*[271]

Depending on how those experiences would be defined, it can just as well be said that atheists can have them, too, and that being religious is no guarantee of having them.

Religion versus Science
Sigmund Freud's main theme in his book *The Future of an Illusion* is the conflict between religion and science as opposite approaches to understanding and relating to the world. A good part of Oskar Pfister's text deals with the same polarity.

It is a strange one. Comparing religion and science as if

---
[270] Ibid., p. 564.
[271] Ibid., p. 576.

interchangeable is questionable, indeed. They are different concepts, different entities, with very little in common. Science is a process by which to explore and explain the world and all its components. It is a method of investigation. Religion, on the other hand, is a way to relate to the world, attaching meaning to it on a personal and social level. It is an attitude towards life. Science is pursued by reason, whereas religion is pursued by emotion.

It is possible to apply science to the phenomenon of religion, its manifestations and doctrines, in order to describe it. But it is not a method by which to discard religion, as if it were a scientific theory proven to be false. Religion is neither constructed by nor dependent on scientific validation. Its claims are held to be true among its devotees, which is not the same as establishing facts. It is admittedly subjective. That is, to a great extent, the point of it.

Judging religion by its scientific accuracy is as irrelevant as judging science from a religious standpoint. Not that it hasn't been done, repeatedly by both. That may be where they actually meet, since it is usually done by evaluating the consequences of them, what they lead to in people's minds and in society. It is also what both Freud and Pfister focus on in their texts.

What Freud means by the illusion is that of religious beliefs, whereas Pfister counters by stating that the blessing of science is just as much an illusion. He puts it rather bluntly, while at the same time showing respect for the pioneer of psychoanalysis:

> *One can forgive such a successful and brilliant pioneer if, at the moment when he attempts to smother religious illusion, he establishes the Messiahship of science, without noticing that in this belief illusion also struts.*[272]

[272] Ibid., p. 570.

Ergo his reversal of Freud's book title from *The Future of an Illusion* to *The Illusion of a Future*. Freud means that the illusion of religion is doomed to disappear in the future, while Pfister insists that it is an illusion to believe religion will perish as science advances and the latter will suffice for people to be content. To him, both are needed.

One of his arguments is that many famous scientists and other admired thinkers were in agreement with religion and science at the same time.[273] He names several of them, such as Descartes, Newton, Darwin, Pasteur, Leibniz, Pascal, Gauss, and even Einstein. But most of those mentioned belonged to a time when Christianity was not only dominant in European culture, but practically compulsory. They may have expressed a different view if they felt at liberty to do so. Even Voltaire treaded quite carefully when speaking about things relating to the dogma of the church.

Pfister neglects the same aspect when discussing the arts. He calls religion the sun that pushes forth the most glorious blossom-life of art and goes on to claim: "All great and powerful art is prayer and an offering before God's throne."[274] Among the artists inspired by Christian feeling he names Leonardo da Vinci and Michelangelo's *Pietà*.[275]

Certainly, religious themes were very common in art works of past centuries, but that was not necessarily from piety of the artist. The church was simply a very wealthy and frequent buyer of art, with a particular taste. Artists could comply or starve, if they were not able to make a living solely from portraits and sculptures of royals and aristocrats.

As for Michelangelo's *Pietà*, its inspiration and sentiment may be any mother grieving her dead son, and Leonardo da Vinci was expressly driven by research into many fields, with the attitude of a scientist also when painting. This is clear in his

---

[273] Ibid., p. 568.

[274] Ibid., p. 575.

[275] Ibid., p. 574.

notebooks, where he discusses many subjects of art and science, but not religion.

That does not mean he was an atheist. It would not only be dangerously blasphemous in his days, but also hard for him to fathom. Without a god, the existence of the world and all its creatures would be difficult to explain before the discoveries by Newton and Darwin. A supreme power was assumed.

On the other hand, it did not mean that artists worked by divine inspiration. Usually, they were not particularly pious. Leonardo had a practical rather than devotional attitude towards art and God's role in it: "Thou, O God, dost sell unto us all good things at the price of labour."[276] That is comparable to the quote accredited to George Bernhard Shaw about artistic creativity being "ninety per cent perspiration, ten per cent inspiration,"[277] as well as Thomas Edison's opinion about genius being 1% inspiration and 99% perspiration.[278]

Christianity as a Cure of Fear

In 1944, sixteen years after the above discussed text, Oskar Pfister published *Das Christentum und die Angst*, which was translated to English four years later as *Christianity and Fear*. The book, spanning almost 600 pages, returns to the same subject — that of Jesus as sort of a psychoanalyst and his doctrine one of freeing people from guilt-induced neurosis.

The English title's "fear" is somewhat misleading. The German word *Angst* can indeed be translated so, but as the text points out, the concept intended is closer to anxiety or for that matter the loanword angst as it is used in English. Simply put, it represents, as Pfister uses it, a persistent trepidation about something that is not a concrete or imminent threat. For the emotional response to a threat that is concrete and imminent,

---

[276] Leonardo da Vinci, *The Notebooks of Leonardo da Vinci*, transl. Edward MacCurdy, New York 1955 (first published in 1939), p. 85.

[277] Arthur Koestler, *The Act of Creation*, New York 1964, p. 120.

[278] quoteinvestigator.com/2012/12/14/genius-ratio/

Pfister uses *Furcht*, which is translated to "dread" in the English version.[279] Another possible translation would be "fright," emphasizing its imminence.

Pfister regards the two terms as describing different emotions, but that can be debated. What they indicate, as he uses them, are different causes or catalysts to an emotion that may essentially be one and the same — the adrenaline induced high-alert response to danger, real or imagined, taking us to the fight-or-flight mode. It is an essential resource for our survival, which is why it can be triggered when no real or imminent threat appears. As the saying goes: better safe than sorry.

The real and imminent threat awakens a response, and when that threat is overcome or avoided, we return to our normal mode. A remaining threat, then, keeps us in the alert mode we experience as trepidation, fear, dread, fright, or whatever we call it. So can the vague impression of a threat we are unable to sufficiently define and therefore also unable to end. If such senses of threat are persistent, according to Pfister, they can lead to neurosis. That is what he sees flawed religions cause. They keep people in a state of fear — fear of a vindictive god, fear of an eternal hell awaiting the deceased, and so on.

Love
Accordingly, his solution is another emotion, namely love. It is the antidote to fear. His primary argument for this is from the Bible, in the First Epistle of John 4:18: "There is no fear in love; but perfect love casteth out fear: because fear hath torment. He that feareth is not made perfect in love." Pfister explains, "fear is thus caused by disturbances of love."[280]

But that is not what the Bible quote says. It does not state what is the cause of fear. It simply says that the presence of one

---

[279] Oskar Pfister, *Christianity and Fear: A Study in History and in the Psychology and Hygiene of Religion*, transl. W. H. Johnston, London 1948 (originally published in German 1944), p. 7.

[280] Ibid., 46.

excludes the other. Where there is fear there cannot be love, and vice versa. It also says that love is the stronger entity. Where it enters, fear dissolves. That means fear is unable to disturb love. It can only remain where love is absent.

Another thing to consider is what may be meant by love — in the Epistle as well as in Pfister's text. That is even more of an enigma than fear. Although it is to Pfister the elixir that can save mankind, he spends significantly less words on it than he does on the concept of fear. He refers to a previous text of his where he defined love, but adds that he wishes to alter it slightly:

> *I have defined love as a sensation resulting from a need and directed towards an object promising satisfaction, the sensation being one of attraction and devotion. To-day, I should prefer to substitute inclination for devotion.*[281]

He points out: "There is no such thing as love without an object." That may be true for what ignites it, but not for the emotion itself. When we love, we tend to expand the delight it inspires to all our surroundings, animate as well as inanimate objects. It is an intoxication without boundaries.

Considering the importance he gives this emotion, his perception of it is surprisingly limited. As an example, he mentions that children love sweet fruit and experience a desire to taste it. That is definitely not to love, but to like. Children know the difference.

He goes on to speak about a higher level love incorporating aesthetic, ethical, religious and intellectual values. Again, that is not relevant to the emotion itself, but rather to how it is defended.

Then he separates love directed to the subject from that to an object. The former is an instrument to increase personal pleasure, which Pfister labels narcissism. The latter is directed

---

[281] Ibid., p. 45.

towards the interest of others and doing everything for them. Another terminology would be selfish and unselfish love.

This may seem like a dismissal of self-love, but in his book Pfister insists repeatedly — in accordance with the famous saying of Jesus to love one's neighbor as oneself — that this love, too, is essential. Rejecting it frequently leads to "a masochistic contraction of the personality."[282]

There is also a third kind of love, again describing who or what is loved rather than the nature of the emotion: the love of God, by which he means the Christian devotion to God as Jesus portrayed him. This was a loving God, and his love was of its very own kind, "the sacred love and kindness which he apprehended to be God's innermost nature."[283] This divine love goes beyond what is fathomable:

> *It cannot be adequately defined in abstract formulae, for it is the very essence, impulse and will of love tending towards the realization of kindness, justice and truth to the utmost of its ability.*

As for the nature of the love possible to express by humans, Pfister discusses the Greek terms *agape* and *eros*. His starting point is the substantial writing on the subject by the Swedish theologian Anders Nygren, who regarded the two kinds of love quite similarly to Pfister — one being selfless and the other selfish, where only the former is the truly Christian kind.[284]

Nygren and Pfister differ in that the latter would not condemn selfish love, and he regards the polarity argued by Nygren as exaggerated. He points out: "Frequently the Greek *eros*

---

[282] Ibid., p. 514.

[283] Ibid., p. 184.

[284] Anders Nygren, *Agape and Eros*, transl. Philip S. Watson, Philadelphia 1953 (originally published in Swedish as *Den kristna kärlekstanken genom tiderna. Eros och Agape*, part I 1930 and part II 1936).

is a descending and selfless love." He finds support for it in Plato's *Symposium*, where it is said about the deity Eros: "He is the oldest of the gods and is for us the source of the highest values."[285]

Indeed, Eros is a deity who represents something far beyond the mere lust that is often linked to him. In the creation story of Hesiod's *Theogony*, Eros is one of the first deities to appear and he is given remarkable traits:

> *Eros, who is the most beautiful among the immortal gods, the limb-melter — he overpowers the mind and the thoughtful counsel of all the gods and of all human beings in their breasts.*[286]

In the original Greek language text of the New Testament, the word *eros* is never used, but so is *agape* frequently, although it is quite rare in classical Greek literature. Therefore, the Christian ideas of the concept have come to dominate the understanding of it as an expression of unconditional love, in particular "the love of God for man and of man for God."[287]

Pfister states that the blessing of love, as Jesus promoted it, surpasses the difference between wanting and giving it, so that the good outcome is still reached:

> *Giving and receiving, desire and attraction, merge together in love.*[288]

To Pfister, Christian love when properly understood as Jesus intended it will liberate people from neurotic fear and

---

[285] Pfister 1948, p. 517.

[286] Hesiod, *Theogony*, transl. Glenn W. Most, Loeb 57, Cambridge Massachusetts 2006, p. 13.

[287] "ἀγάπη," Henry George Liddell & Robert Scott, *An Intermediate Greek-English Lexicon*, Oxford 1889, p. 4.

[288] Pfister 1948, p. 518.

make them able to feel and act in accordance with *agape*. In a therapeutic term, it will cure them.

Hygiene

The curing of Christian minds through a proper understanding and committing to the love of which Jesus spoke, Pfister speaks of as a religious hygiene. The word hygiene has some complicated connotations, especially in the time and place of Pfister's book, which was 1944 in Europe.

That was the year before World War II ended and the concentration camps were displayed to a whole world aghast. They showed the monstrous Nazi application of eugenics, labeled racial hygiene. In 1944 the concentration camps were not yet well known, but the grotesque ideas of racial hygiene were.

Oskar Pfister must have been aware of them, but his use of the term hygiene cannot be interpreted as him agreeing with that dreadful application. It is just unfortunate, especially when used in a social setting and not just in the medical sense of personal preventive healthcare. He speaks of the hygiene of religion serving "the cause of social and national hygiene,"[289] and points out that "in the schools too hygiene cannot be neglected."[290] By the end of his book, he states:

> *The great problems of personality and civilization which must be solved if mankind is to be saved can be settled only by the aid of a scientifically applied hygiene fostering a vigorous way of life based on love in the Christian sense and making this, not in theory but in practice, its ultimate objective.*[291]

That attitude, though promoting love, has an uncompromising tone of justification not enough distanced from the

[289] Ibid., p. 26.
[290] Ibid., p. 11.
[291] Ibid., p. 574.

rhetoric of eugenics. The idea that one solution would fit all mankind is in itself questionable, indeed, and not less so when "based on methods of depth psychology and mental hygiene."[292]

In addition, Pfister's conviction that it has to be Christianity doing the job, no other religion being apt to it, and his interpretation of proper Christianity at that, makes the impression of intolerance pungent. In 1944, this narrow perspective might have been somewhat understandable, but the English translation was published – under his supervision — in 1948, when the dreadful consequences of intolerance were obvious to everyone.

What made him blind to this insensitivity was probably his conviction that his message dealt with the sacred, a divine perspective far above the turmoil of secular events. Conviction is known to cause loss of clear sight, and religious conviction is definitely no exception.

Much like his previous texts discussed above, *Christianity and Fear* incorporates psychoanalytical theories and methods, but its perspective is mainly theological. This is a man of the cloth trying his best to keep his religion relevant in a changing world, using novel theories of psychology to make his case. His major shortcoming is that he demands of his findings to propagate his own faith, which takes its toll on his reasoning.

Freud could have told him, and probably did as best he could in their correspondence, that religion and psychoanalysis are no perfect match. Already the fundamental principle of the Oedipus complex should have told him that. It presents religion as a consequence of guilt feelings, not at all a solution to them.

---

[292] Ibid., p. 11.

Theodor Reik

Theodor Reik (1888-1969) was a psychology student at the University of Vienna when he in 1910 met Sigmund Freud, who was a professor of neurology there. Reik became his student and they remained on good terms until Freud's death. Reik got his PhD in psychology in 1912, with a dissertation on Gustave Flaubert's *The Temptation of Saint Anthony*, where he applied a psychoanalytical method.

In 1928 he moved to Berlin and set up a practice, but as Nazism rose, he moved to the Netherlands and in 1938 to New York, where he established a clinic and remained for the rest of his life.

His writing on mythology is limited. Discussed below is a book on ritual, *Ritual: Psycho-Analytic Studies*, which was the first in what was supposed to be a series of books on problems in the psychology of religion, but no additional volumes were released. The volume on ritual was originally published in 1919, with a preface by Freud, and a revised second edition came in 1928. The English translation from 1931 is based on the second edition.

Psychoanalytic Studies of Ritual

The book is a collection of four lectures held between 1914 and 1919 at the Berlin and Vienna branches of the International Psycho-Analytical Association. The four rituals discussed in the lectures are couvade, puberty rites, and the Jewish rites involving *Kol Nidre* and the *Shofar*. Since myths are only indirectly discussed, the treatment of his book will be limited to the first two rituals.

Still, they do present some psychoanalytical perspectives on religion and mythology. Reik is not modest about what the discipline can reveal simply by exposing "those unconscious impulses, to which analysis points as determining the genesis and essence of religion."[293] That would not leave much undone.

Regarding myth, Reik states firmly that it is older than religion, and "one of the oldest wish-compensations of mankind in its eternal struggle with external and internal forces."[294] Therefore, myth is "of the highest importance for our understanding of the first psychological conflicts of primitive people." Although it precedes religion, it allies itself with religious cults, sharing their history:

> *The same affects, wishes and tendencies are operative in myth and in religion and can be recognised as the unconscious roots of both those products of the mass-psyche.*

Myth also has the advantage of being easier to decipher as an expression of the unconsciously preserved memories and their repression:

> *It must indeed be recognised that myth, in its original state, preserves in a far less disguised form the memory of those events which led to the institution of religion than do the other forms of phantasy formation in which the share of unconscious powers and forces of repression can be demonstrated.*

It should be noted that he refers to the original state of myth, which is something he and his fellow Freudians reach by psychoanalytical theory about the true meaning of the content. Before psychoanalysis, "science had no means of recognising all the later distortions and alterations of the myth and of laying bare its hidden and original meaning." He states with

---

[293] Theodor Reik, *Ritual: Psycho-Analytic Studies* (*Das Ritual: Psychoanalytische Studien*, 1928, revised edition of *Probleme der Religionspsychologie*, 1919), transl. Douglas Bryan, London 1931, p. 14.

[294] Ibid., p. 18.

a boldness so often shared by his fellow psychoanalysts: "Since psycho-analysis has succeeded in interpreting myths, their significance in folk-psychology has been more and more recognised."[295]

The events leading to the formation of religion he speaks of are those suggested by Freud as the prehistoric causes of the Oedipus complex. As stated both by him and in Freud's preface, Reik applies his teacher's *Totem and Taboo* to the analysis of rituals, and quite slavishly at that.[296] Reik's praise of the book is monumental. He describes it as "hitherto the most important work of the kind, and one that will always remain the standard illustration of what psycho-analysis can perform in the sphere of mental science."

Although stressing the importance and antiquity of myth, Reik finds ritual particularly suitable for psychoanalytical approach, since it is an active expression of religion:

> *The character of action which is such a marked feature of ritual may be more profitably investigated psycho-analytically than the ideas, commands, prohibition, dogmas and complicated sentiments, which have later become the chief content of religion.*[297]

The added bonus is that whereas dogmas change through time, "religious customs show a remarkable resistance to external influences."[298] The rituals tend to stay the same in spite of social changes. Not all of them, certainly, as is evident regarding the rites he describes in the book, but many traditional behaviors rooted in ancient beliefs remain even when those beliefs have all but vanished.

The more difficult question is to what extent they were

---

[295] Ibid., pp. 18f.

[296] Ibid., pp. 15 and 10.

[297] Ibid., p. 16.

[298] Ibid., p. 17.

firm beliefs to begin with. Some rituals may have been consciously composed fantasy projects from the start, with or without a belief backing them up. For example, the modern way of celebrating Christmas would be misunderstood if future researchers regarded it as proof of our belief in Santa Claus.

Couvade

Couvade is the term for the tradition in some cultures of the father restricting his behavior during and after the mother gives birth to their child. Although the term existed beforehand, E. B. Tylor introduced it to anthropology in 1865.[299] He translates it as "hatching." While the mother is in labor or approaching it or right after it, the father stays passive in bed as if the labor was his. In some cases, he also has dietary restrictions and is forbidden certain forceful activities, such as hunting big animals.

A modern use of the term is *couvade syndrome*, which is the sympathetic pregnancy experienced by some fathers. But in his lecture on the subject from 1914, *Couvade and the Psychogenesis of the Fear of Retaliation*, Reik refers to the old ritual.

Tylor and others explained the custom as an example of sympathetic magic, aimed at protecting the baby and easing the ordeal of the mother. Reik, in his psychoanalytical explanation, actually reverses it.

He sees the father's behavior as based on the hidden unconscious wish to increase the mother's pain and even to kill the baby.[300] The father struggles unconsciously with these wishes, resulting in him masochistically striking himself with them, punishing himself with the pains. Thereby, his tender impulses have won over the hostile ones:

---

[299] Edward Burnet Tylor, *Researches Into the Early History of Mankind and the Development of Civilization*, London 1865, p. 288.

[300] Reik, *Ritual*, p. 50.

> *Having assumed that malevolent wishes of a sadistic nature are awakened in the husband, it follows that the suppression of these wishes will bring about a relatively increased intensity of the masochistic instinctual components. In the play of forces between sadistic and masochistic tendencies, and in the struggle between hostile and tender impulses, the latter, which alone could become conscious, have obtained the victory.*[301]

The father's hostility is caused by his sexual frustration from not having access to the mother in the late stage of pregnancy, at the same time as her increased helplessness through her condition is a constant temptation to him.[302] The consequence is his rising aversion towards her:

> *His inhibited libido joins itself to those inborn sadistic instinctual components which the woman's condition brings to the fore and is turned into latent hate against her.*[303]

Therefore, the couvade is not really about easing the woman's labor pains, though that is assumed even by those following the custom. Its real social purpose is to protect the woman against the latent hostility and sexual aggression of the man.[304]

It is the dietary couvade that reveals repressed hostile impulses towards the child.[305] Again Reik uses a reversal. The restrictions on food and activity were supposed to be sympathetic magic for the protection of the child, and ignoring them might harm it, but: "The feared consequence of doing the for-

---

[301] Ibid., p. 53.
[302] Ibid., p. 54.
[303] Ibid., p. 55.
[304] Ibid., p. 56.
[305] Ibid., p. 59.

bidden things — the child would become sick and die — was once the desired consequence of the breaking out of hostile impulses."[306] Behind it all is the father's death wish towards the child. Reik makes a quick and frightful sketch of the mentality of the primitive human able to host such thoughts:

> *One cannot conceive him having much fatherly tenderness. A strange being has come into his home and he feels no pleasure in supporting the little creature. On the contrary, he feels impelled to kill and devour the child.*

Leaving aside the questionable prejudice about primitive man fostering such feelings against his child whereas presumably civilized man would not, Reik goes on with an even more alarming statement, "to-day the killing and eating of children is not unknown among certain peoples."[307] He gives no source to the claim.

If that has any truth at all, it is certainly not "peoples" but individuals all on their own. Even in mythology it is depicted as a disgusting deed by deities soon suffering the punishment. Cronus (Saturn) is a famous example. And Jonathan Swift's *A Modest Proposal* from 1729 is, of course, nothing but a satire.

Reik has an explanation to the father's vile hostility towards the child, which is at least equally far-fetched, though quite familiar to Freudian psychoanalysis. It is the Oedipus complex again. The primeval revolt against the father, relived in the minds of every following generation, ends up with the son becoming a father: "The son, who in childhood had wished the death of the father in order to take his place with the mother, has now himself become a man and father."[308]

That means he would fear his son repeating the deed with him, but Reik insists on another complication: "In the belief of

---

[306] Ibid., p. 60.
[307] Ibid., p. 61.
[308] Ibid., p. 75.

the savage people the child represents not the rebirth of its father, but the rebirth of its father's father."[309] No doubt, that increases the fear of retaliation. His son is none other than his own father, whom he revolted against.

> *We see also more precisely why he kills the child; he carries out once more the impulse of hate towards the deceased father; he kills once more his own father in the child.*[310]

But as civilization proceeded the child was replaced by a sacrificial animal. By time, even that was not allowed:

> *The taboo was made stricter, and finally extended so far that the killing of the animals at the period when the man became a father was also included in it. Here we perceive the origin of the rules of the dietetic couvade.*[311]

The fasting prohibition "originally only referred to the devouring of the child."[312]

Fathers killing their children are not unheard of in human history and in the present, but that does not mean it has ever been a strong urge in men. If so, it would have put a quick end to the procreation of our species. Even more absurd is the claim that rituals were needed to hinder fathers from eating their offspring.

Reik is led astray by what he wants to find, whatever detours it makes him take. That is a streak he shares with his psychoanalytical colleagues. Already in choosing his subject he has obviously been attracted by the components of the Oedipus complex — the father, the mother, and the son. His commitment to Freud's doctrine and *Totem and Taboo* did the rest.

---

[309] Ibid., p. 79.
[310] Ibid., p. 78.
[311] Ibid., p. 81.
[312] Ibid., p. 83.

Reik's prejudiced account of the ritual and how it was played out in different cultures makes it difficult to get enough of a clear picture of it to suggest other explanations. But Tylor and others have already suggested sympathetic magic, and that would lend itself to a less complicated explanation.

Then the father lying in bed would really be an act of trying to ease the pain of the mother by accepting it to transfer into him during her labor, and maybe an act of transferring his power to her when he remained in bed after she had left it. Dietary restrictions would be due to the belief that father and child were connected and some food was regarded as harmful to the newborn, so the father avoided it to spare the child. This was also implied in some of the sources Reik used, though he brushed it aside.

An interesting aspect is the need for passivity of the father, disallowing him to handle weapons or chasing big game, and so on. That would be taken care of by him remaining in bed, so it must belong to other versions of the couvade. Invoking personal powers as well as challenging fierce beasts would, if father and child were connected, intimidate and frighten the latter.

There is also a possibility of the simple consideration that the father should not hurry to take risks when he had a newborn to protect.

Infanticide versus the Oedipus Complex
There is no denying that fathers, like any male adults, have been more of a threat to infants than the mothers. History has proven it often enough, among both humans and many other animals. It would worry both a mother and an infant if the father started swinging a sword right after delivery.

Still, it is doubtful that a brutal father would settle for a ritual doing the opposite of his intention. He might instead feel better raging after big prey.

If other primates are comparable to humans in this context, infanticide is known among 35 of those species. They are not exclusively done by males or targeted at male infants, nor are they necessarily done in order to diminish competition for reproduction, but such cases do exist.[313] What is particularly rare among primates, though, is paternal and maternal infanticide.

Humans may be the primates most inclined to infanticide of their own offspring, but it is definitely not a common occurrence. Not enough, really, for a complicated ritual to be formed and continued for multiple generations. What would make more sense, for humans as well as other primates, is a ritual to protect the newborn from other adults — male and female — than the parents. But that would be out of the scope of Freudian doctrine, which is based on the Oedipus complex.

There are some intriguing similarities between male infanticide among mammals and the Oedipus complex. They involve a mortal drama between male, female, and child, with sexuality at the root. Males do it mostly to get access to impregnate the female. This is strongly supported by the fact that the behavior is not found among mammals with seasonal reproduction.[314]

Only in species where the female can give birth the year around would the strategy make any sense, since it would speed up the possibility of impregnating her. It should be noted, though, that the males avoid killing their own offspring.

Although it is not a behavior involving father and son, it is one where males compete ferociously about access to the females for sexual purposes. This makes Reik's insistence on the Oedipus complex even more far-fetched. It has nothing to do with patricide or the father's father, but with removing another male's child to gain access to the mother — in order for the aggressor to produce his own children with her. That is among

---

[313] Sara Alvarez et al., "Male-directed infanticide in spider monkeys," *Primates*, volume 56:2, 2015, p. 173 (springer.com).

[314] Will Dunham, "Infanticide common among adult males in many mammal species," *Reuters*, November 13, 2014 (reuters.com).

many primates the real threat, maybe also in a distant past among humans.

Psychoanalysts have focused on the son's envy of his father and the wish to take his place, already from infancy. What seems more plausible is the fear of the father. Paternal infanticide may be very rare, but the father's dominance and superior strength are not. The child's fate is helplessly in the hands of the father, not only in distant history. Children have good reason to regard their fathers as threats.

Gender roles were quite clear in the society of Freud and his pupils. The father was the master, also the punisher, especially when the punishment was to be physical. A stern father would certainly by time cause vindictive longings in his son, but that would grow out of the torment of living in fear of him. The mother had little to do with it, except in cases of the son's frustration over her inability to protect him from the father.

Nevertheless, there is reason to contemplate the tense relation between adult and infant males in both past and present societies, and the sexual implications of them. There is just no overwhelming support for describing it all with the theory of the Oedipus complex. Other explanations are nearer at hand.

Oedipal Puberty Rites

In 1915, at the Vienna Psycho-Analytical Society, Theodor Reik gave a lecture on a similar theme to the above: *The Puberty Rites of Savages: Some Parallels between the Mental Life of Savages and of Neurotics*. Again, he used Freud's *Totem and Taboo* to find the Oedipus complex at work in rituals, this time the rites of passage at puberty.

With the term savages, he refers to hunter-gatherer societies, using an abundance of ethnological material from James G. Frazer and others. He does not deny that those societies have evolved through time, but he regards them as primitive in comparison to the ones of the industrialized parts of the world.

As for the comparison to neurotics, he does it scarcely and

superfluously. The bulk of his arguments are based on ethnographic material about the so-called primitives.

There are two puberty rites his text focuses on — the circumcision and the ostensible death and resurrection of boys. He explains them, of course, as expressions of the Oedipus complex. They are to discourage the adolescents from killing their fathers and lusting after their mothers.

The circumcision is a symbol of castration, intended to lessen the sexual drive of the boys, so that they will be able to resist their desires for their mothers, since "circumcision represents a castration equivalent and supports in the most effective way the prohibition against incest."[315]

The ordeal of the ritualized death, which involves an imaginary monster Reik claims to represent the grandfather,[316] is the way of the fathers to scare the boys from trying to harm them:

The rite of being devoured by the monster is a threat of death and a psychic reaction to the youth's unconscious intention to murder his father.[317]

According to Reik, the animosity between the generations of males goes as far as to the appetite for cannibalism, which thankfully diminishes by age:

The temptation to kill and devour the father which originates unconsciously from the Oedipus complex is natural to the young and passionate man; the older he becomes, the stronger is his tendency to identify himself with his own father, and the weaker becomes the temptation.[318]

---

[315] Reik, *Ritual*, p. 105.

[316] Ibid., p. 99.

[317] Ibid., p. 106.

[318] Ibid., p. 116.

Reik shows no hesitation about his explanations. Instead, he even scorns ethnologists and anthropologists for not realizing the same.[319]

He also takes a shot at Carl G. Jung for having presented an alternative to the Oedipus complex in his 1912 book *Wandlungen und Symbole der Libido* (published in English in 1916 as *Psychology of the Unconscious*), where the childish urge is instead described as an unconscious wish to return to the safety of the mother's womb and then to be reborn from it. To Reik, this is pure nonsense:

> *Every psychological investigation that is not merely superficial is able to prove that such an idea represents neither the essential nor the effective thing.*[320]

Reik's critique of Jung can be described with the psychological term projection. The proof he presents for his own theory is questionable, too, to say the least. He is certainly no friend of Ockham's razor. Simpler explanations to these rites he either omits or discards.

He accepts neither the opinions of the anthropologists whose material he is using, nor the answers given by the people whose rituals are described.

He dismisses the reason for circumcision given by anthropologists and "primitives" alike, "that it is an operation for facilitating sexual intercourse and increasing its pleasures."[321] The real functions of the rites are unconscious and therefore hidden from the conscious minds of their practitioners:

> *Unconsciously circumcision and the various cruelties practised on the youths signify the suppression of their sexual and aggressive impulses; consciously primitive peoples*

---

[319] Ibid., pp. 117, footnote, and 123.
[320] Ibid., p. 148.
[321] Ibid., pp. 124f.

regard these procedures as institutions for the actual promotion of those impulses.[322]

A Rite of Passage

In his Freudian conviction, Reik refused to even consider other likely explanations, although they were accessible in the material he had at his disposal. He would have done well to start by putting this rite in relation to the other rites of passage[323] that are prominent and comparable in any society — past and present.

There are four major passages or transformations humans go through in a lifetime: birth, puberty, procreation, and death. Each has a significant rite connected to it. In the Christian society they are the baptism, the confirmation, the wedding, and the funeral. There is little chance of understanding the emergence and components of one of these rites without seeing its relation to the other three.

Obviously, the key is in the word "passage" used in anthropology for these rites. They are performed when life changes significantly from one situation to another, intended to prepare for as well as celebrate these changes.

Newborns are baptized to be introduced into the community and receive their protection, and at the other end the dead are celebrated for their contribution and prepared for whatever is believed to come next. The wedding is an invitation for the couple to procreate, and to discourage others from pursuing them for the same purpose. The confirmation is a call to leave childhood and enter the world of the adults.

Puberty is certainly a drastic change, physically as well as psychologically, in no need of the Oedipus complex to deserve a rite. Also, the components of the rite as described by Reik are easy to connect to the passage in question.

---

[322] Ibid., p. 117.

[323] The concept was introduced by the ethnographer Arnold van Gennep in *Les rites de passage*, 1909.

The coming-of-age passage rite has the function of letting both the boy and his community know that now he has become a man. His childhood is over. That is a death and a rebirth — the child dies and the man is born. It also means that he detaches from his mother to make close bonds with the other men, which Reik instead explains as a measure to the prevention of incest.[324]

This sheds light on the occurrence in the ritual of the boy behaving as if completely forgetful of his past when returning from the ordeal, which Reik described as peculiar: "The youths behave as though they had forgotten their previous life."[325] It is part of the transformation. The life of the child is to be forgotten, because there is a new life to live.

Reik's explanation to this momentary amnesia is as elaborate as it is predictable:

The youths are to forget, or better, 'repress' what constituted hitherto their chief desire, namely, to put the father out of the way and take his place with the mother.[326]

What may seem even more peculiar is the circumcision. It is hardly to be seen as a castration. What would be the point of celebrating sexual maturity by ending it, symbolically or otherwise? The focus on this part of the male anatomy is understandable, since it is very much what the passage is all about. In addition, the explanation of the natives, mentioned above, should be given some credit. Health and hygiene intentions are also probable.

Its role as an ingredient in a rite of passage is indicated also by the Jewish practice of performing circumcision soon after birth, which is of course another most significant passage. Although a Jew himself, Reik does not discuss that timing of

---

[324] Reik, *Ritual*, p. 145.
[325] Ibid., p. 126.
[326] Ibid., p. 137.

the procedure in his text. It would put his oedipal explanation into question, since newborns are no threats to their fathers, nor are they likely to remember the lesson until puberty.

There is something more with the circumcision, worthy of considering. It is the bleeding and its correspondence to the bleeding that signals the sexual maturity of girls. So, both sexes are introduced to their adult lives by the same bodily fluid, which is a vital and highly symbolic one, also in this case coming from their respective reproductive organs.

Reik makes no mention of female puberty rites and he might not even have asked himself if they exist at all among natives. That would complicate matters for his understanding of the male rite and even of the Oedipus complex as a whole. Freud denied that it had a female counterpart, suggested by Jung as the Electra complex. The loyal Reik would not question Freud's view. On the other hand, he was hardly ignorant of the fact that in Western society, all four rites of passage mentioned are done for both genders.

He had an excuse in the case of rites within hunter-gatherer societies, since the ethnographic material at the time was very scarce indeed with reports on female rites — simply because the field research was done by men. They would not have access to female rites, nor were they probably aware of their existence.

Reik could have surmised the hidden existence of a female counterpart to the male rites, since he was aware of women being strictly excluded from the latter.[327] He also gives other examples of the male world that women were forbidden to enter. The guess that the same would be true for the opposite is not far off.

Instead, Reik mentions the male secret societies spread among the "primitive" peoples of the world, as reported by the 19th century German ethnologist Heinrich Schurtz:

---

[327] Ibid., p. 96.

> *He shows very clearly that the men's societies are 'the real bearers of almost all higher development'.*[328]

That is another claim which must be questioned. For both Reik and Schurtz, their own gender dimmed their eyes. It was not uncommon at that time.

Of course, there are and have been many examples of female puberty rites around the world, often excluding men completely from participating. The first menstruation, *menarche*, is a passage of great significance in any culture, as it is to any girl.

---

[328] Ibid., p. 150.

Géza Róheim

Géza Róheim (1891-1953), a Hungarian psychoanalyst and anthropologist, became the first professor of anthropology at the University of Budapest in 1919 and was active in the psychoanalytical institute of the same city, after having been analyzed by Sándor Ferenczi, one of Freud's closest pupils.

In 1928 Róheim made a field expedition to study natives in Australia from the perspective of psychoanalytic anthropology. At the outbreak of World War II in 1939, Róheim had to flee to New York, where he spent the rest of his life.

He remained an advocate of the Freudian doctrine of the primal *Cyclopean family*[329] and the Oedipus complex, although altering some aspects of it in accordance with his anthropological conclusions. By time, he tended to turn his attention more to the importance of the extended childhood of the human species and its consequences on the human psyche and society.

Primitive Man and Environment

For more purposes than the study of mythology, psychoanalysts have frequently used anthropological sources, though not always sufficiently familiar with that discipline. It is quite refreshing to read someone who was.

Géza Róheim reasons straightforwardly about Freudian concepts and explains them as consequences of biological conditions and not only some mysterious workings of the darker corners of our minds. This can be seen in his 1921 article "Primitive Man and Environment," published in *The International Journal of Psycho-Analysis*, where he connects psychoanalytical principles to anthropogeography.

With examples from anthropological reports about na-

---

[329] A primal herd consisting of but one adult male with several female mates, where other males are expelled at a young age, as suggested by James Jasper Atkinson. Lang & Atkinson 1903, p. 230.

tives in Australia and elsewhere, he sets out to show that a number of beliefs are expressions "in the language of unconscious symbolism of the *unity which connects human life with Nature.*"[330] Therefore, "all myths are true, only we must know the way to read them."[331]

Some of that reading has to be quite imaginative. Róheim claims that most primitive people unconsciously regarded the world around them as a second womb, which he explains: "If man is born with the concept of space it is natural to assume that he must have derived it from his own prenatal experience."[332] This influenced mythology:

> *The cosmogonical myths which relate how in the beginning Father Sky was in close embrace with Mother Earth so that there was no room left for their children, and how these lifted the sky to its present height, contain (besides the Oedipus-complex) an "auto-symbolical" or "functional" account of the origin of the space concept which was first received in the cramped position of the embryo, the experiences of which were then projected into the universe.*

This prenatal perception of space Róheim also finds expressed in the use of caves as living quarters, which were "unconscious projections of the womb into the environment,"[333] and in the fetus-like position of buried corpses. The latter he explains as a belief in reincarnation, so that the dead were returned to a womb of sorts in order to be reborn.[334] For the same reason, some tribes buried their dead at the place of their birth. Mother Earth was the symbolic substitute for the real mother.

---

[330] Géza Róheim, "Primitive Man and Environment," *The International Journal of Psycho-Analysis*, volume II:2 1921, p. 158. The italics are his.

[331] Ibid., p. 177.

[332] Ibid., p. 163, footnote.

[333] Ibid., p. 164.

[334] Ibid., pp. 166f.

He moves on to discuss the spatial concepts of high and low in the human mind and culture. Some are above and looked up to, often the elders whose privileges stem from "an infantile mental attitude towards the father."[335] Children look up to their fathers, literally, and this sense of inferiority remains with them. Furthermore, "these same concepts radiate into space and call forth the concepts of a heaven and an underworld (Hell)."

This division of heaven and hell is also expressed in the body of the human being, from the head to the lower cavities.[336] It can also be seen as the conscious personality and the depth of the unconscious. All is due to the psychological mechanism of reversal:

It is not certain regions of the human body that are under the influence of cosmic regions, it is rather the organism of man which determines, not of course the real state of things in the universe, but man's ideas of the Above and the Below.

Although not all of his conclusions are equally convincing, Róheim's ambition to include the physical basics of the human being and the environment, when explaining the mysteries of the human mind, is commendable.

For example, it is far more conceivable that children's perception of their parents is based on such obvious things as their superior size and might, than oedipal urges. Only by growing up to equal measures are the children able to break free of this inferiority, and it is precisely what they eventually do.

But childhood certainly makes its marks in the memory and the emotions. It is well known to play an important part in how we perceive and relate to the world also as adults.

---

[335] Ibid., p. 175.
[336] Ibid., pp. 177f.

The Eternal Ones of the Dream

Géza Róheim made frequent use of the Australian natives in his writing on psychoanalytic anthropology, both before and after his field work with them in 1928. Doing so again in 1945 with *The Eternal Ones of the Dream*, he used both his own findings and those of other writers, who were almost exclusively anthropologists. The book's subtitle is self-explanatory: *A Psychoanalytic Interpretation of Australian Myth and Ritual*.

The myths and rituals interpreted by Róheim are the ones relating to the initiation of boys into manhood, where circumcision is at the core. All through the book, the myths are described as subordinate to the rites and lacking meaning outside of their ritual context. By the myths associated with them, the rites are confirmed and explained. Therefore, Róheim's interpretation of those myths is closely limited to their ritual functions. They are interdependent.

His psychoanalytical understanding of these rites and the myths connected to them is the male rivalry described in the Oedipus complex. The boys are removed from the embrace of their mothers to join with the men, at the same time as they are forcefully intimidated, so as not to fight them. The circumcision is a symbol of castration and therefore a threat of it. At the same time, the procedure is in itself a symbolic separation from the mothers.

Róheim's analysis is complicated and the particulars of the rites and their myths are given more than one symbolic meaning, sometimes contradictory. Usually, he sees one meaning more or less apparent to the natives and another unconscious meaning hiding beneath it, of which they are not aware.

Through his text there is a mixture of psychoanalytic and anthropological or anthropogeographical perspectives on the customs of the Australian natives, which are at best possible to see as parallel. But they often raise the question of how far Róheim would come if he had omitted psychoanalysis completely in his interpretation. In such passages of the text, he tends to make more sense.

For example, he explains that the Murngin (nowadays called Yolngu) population of north-eastern Australia thrives in the dry period and suffers in the extremely rainy one. It is mirrored in their mythology: "The great primeval flood is merely a dramatic enlargement of what takes place every year."[337] The symbolism created from these annual changes reflects the opposites:

> *Myth therefore identifies the season of plenty with the nourishing mother and the season of scarcity with the aggressive, copulating father.*

For the natives of Central Australia, on the other hand, the situation is reversed. They find food in the rainy period but starve in the dry one. Accordingly, they do not celebrate the drought but the rain, and welcome the lightning as a promise of rain, where "the waters are represented by a swallowing and yet beneficial serpent."[338]

That makes sense, without any unconscious interference. What is beneficial is celebrated, and what is detrimental is feared. No need for Oedipus.

As for the intriguing title of Róheim's book, *The Eternal Ones of the Dream*, it is derived from the Aboriginal word *altjira*, which means, "(a) a dream, (b) beings who appear in the dream, and (c) a narrative with a happy end (folk-tale)."[339] It refers to the distant past of the dream time, when the mythical ancestors lived.

The concept of the distant past as a dream time is ingenious. We can all relate to it, even in our short individual lifetimes. Distant memories get hidden in a thickening mist, becoming more and more like dreams, which are difficult to re-

---

[337] Géza Róheim, *The Eternal Ones of the Dream: A Psychoanalytic Interpretation of Australian Myth and Ritual*, New York 1945, p. 245.

[338] Ibid., p. 247.

[339] Ibid., p. 210.

member after waking up. It is a poetic description, and yet spot on. Also, it focuses on the true big mystery of the mind — its ability to create dreams.

What the expression is likely to suggest is that the distant past, which no one alive now has experienced, is as elusive and uncertain as a dream. To Róheim, though, it represents a denial of both mothers and fathers:

> *The eternal ones of the dream are those who have had no mother; they originated of themselves. Their immortality is a denial of separation anxiety. In their origin myths fully-formed spirit children emerge from pouches carried by the ancestors. In one sense this is a denial of fatherhood (Oedipus complex) but in another sense a denial of motherhood, with the mythical being and the pouch replacing the mother.*[340]

This mythical component of the eternals is connected to the problems of dealing with growing up and the illusion of living forever:

> *In the eternal ones of the dream it is we who deny decay and aggression and object-loss, and who guard eternal youth and reunion with the mother.*[341]

That might be true as well, although Róheim has not really proven it. Our inescapable death is a complication for us all, and has been so for as long as it has been known to our species. It has infiltrated every mythology and ritual, regardless of their pronounced subject or purpose. Still, neither Oedipus nor his mother and father are necessary to explain it.

---

[340] Ibid., p. 222.
[341] Ibid., pp. 249f.

Always Oedipus

Were it not for Róheim's persistent return to the Oedipus complex in just about every explanation of myth, ritual, and religion, his discussion on those matters would have been less absurd. But he seemed unable to reach any other conclusion, staying loyal to Freud's paradigm even past his master's death, as can be seen in his 1945 book *The Eternal Ones of the Dream*, discussed above.

Róheim also found the Oedipus complex behind the very origin of religion and the gods, even the formation of society:

> *The Oedipus complex is not a "survival" of the primal-horde but, on the contrary, the primal-horde itself is to be regarded as an early form of social organization arising from the eternally human Oedipus complex.*[342]

The reason for this, according to Róheim, is the extended duration of human childhood, and the series of libidinal traumata it has to endure for so long. Therefore, he is confident to assume that mankind evolved through the repression and sublimation of infantile traumata. This extended infancy also explains our need for supernatural beings, both demons and benevolent spirits:[343]

> *In other words, demons originate because the parents are not as evil as they appear to the child in the light of the primal scene, and doubles and benevolent spirits originate because the parents are not as good as sublimation would have them. The first step denied reality, the second accepted it.*

---

[342] "Primitive High Gods," Géza Róheim, *The Panic of the Gods and Other Essays*, New York 1972, p. 108. Originally published in *The Psychoanalytic Quarterly*, vol. 3 no. 1, 1934.

[343] Ibid., pp. 117f.

Summing up clearly and precisely Christian dogma, he is well aware of the fact that its concept of religion is far from the only one in the world:

The idea of a benevolent and omnipotent father, of a great creator in the sky, who takes care of his children if they behave well and punishes them for sinful conduct, and the notion of a future world in which the good are rewarded and the wicked punished, have not been evolved by such people as the Central Australians and cannot be regarded as the only religion mankind has ever had.[344]

Yet, he uses the same Oedipus recipe to explain them all. The difference he sees is that civilization has increased the repression of natural urges, and his wording indicates that it is not completely fortunate:

Unluckily however we have a superego in our mental makeup, a principle in us that is opposed to life and pleasure, and as mankind grows in age it renounces more and more of the original impulses.[345]

Róheim sees it as death claiming its own. Still, it is not all dark:

But the pendulum sways to and fro and in Christianity we have a creed in which God and religion are equated with love, that is, with Eros in its sublimated aspects.

A couple of years before his death, he wrote the essay "The Panic of the Gods," in which he argued again for the Oedipus complex manifesting in mythology, even being the cause

---

[344] "Animism and Religion," ibid., pp. 121f. Originally published in *The Psychoanalytic Quarterly*, vol. 1, 1932.

[345] Ibid., p. 168.

of it. He was nothing if not persistent. He swiftly dismissed alternative theories, such as those in anthropology and Jungian psychology,[346] ending the text with this conclusion:

> Myth is created by the individual: *the group only rewrites it, modifies it, etc.: first taking shape in the form of a dream, the myth reflects a conflict in the development of every individual — that of growing up; hence the hero of the story is genital libido.*[347]

It is true that any myth must initially have begun with the imagination of one individual, but it would have reached nowhere without the adaption — and modifications — in the society where it was transmitted. And there are so many myths with very different plots and characters, they cannot all be explained with the same simple formula.

Actually, just like his teacher Freud, Róheim fails to prove that the Oedipal complex is at the root of any one of them. But they were too stubborn to even seriously and fairly consider other theories. There must be a term in Freudian psychopathology for such behavior.

---

[346] "The Panic of the Gods," ibid., pp. 218f. Originally published in *The Psychoanalytic Quarterly*, vol. 21, no. 1, 1952.

[347] Ibid., p. 220.

Helene Deutsch

Helene Deutsch (1884-1982) was one of the first and one of the few women to get a noticed position in the psychoanalytic movement. Born in Galicia, she enrolled in medical studies 1907 at the university of Vienna, remaining there for several years working at a clinic. In 1916, she read Freud's *Interpretation of Dreams*, which made her attracted to psychoanalysis.

She was analyzed by Freud and also by Karl Abraham, becoming in 1918 the second woman to be admitted to the Vienna Psychoanalytic Society. The first one was Hermine Hug-Hellmuth, who was also the first child psychoanalyst. In 1935, Deutsch moved to the United States, where she remained for the rest of her long life.

She stayed expressly loyal to Freud all her life, but that did not stop her from venturing into her own theories, sometimes deviating slightly from those of Freud, though remaining within the paradigm of psychoanalysis. The main portion of her writing deals with the psychology of women, which was treated sparsely by Freud and most of his followers. As for the subject of mythology, she dedicated one book to the myths of Dionysus and Apollo rather late in her professional life — *A Psychoanalytic Study of the Myth of Dionysus and Apollo*, published in 1969.

Though the two main characters of her book are men, the theme is their relation to their mothers, which is confirmed already by the subtitle *Two Variants of the Son-Mother Relationship*. Those are indeed opposite variants, where Dionysus is portrayed as saving his mother and Apollo as killing mothers. The Oedipus complex, so dear to Freud, she dismisses as irrelevant here:

> *The fact that the assumed psychological intrusion of another Greek figure, Oedipus, into the family life of Dionysus and Apollo seems not to be of consequence makes my*

concentration on the son-mother relationship less complicated.[348]

That might have upset Freud, had he not been dead for 30 years when this book was published.

Dionysus Saving his Mother

Deutsch starts her chapter about Dionysus by praising his contributions to agriculture, especially that of wine, and to "the emancipation of mortal women."[349] Therefore his statue should be in every agricultural organization and at the entrance to girls' dormitories, but with a distinct note that "the statue is not to commemorate Dionysus's orgastic rites."

In order to find the rationality behind the irrational nonsense of the myth, and understand its meaning, she applies psychoanalysis:

> *In my approach to this myth, which I consider to be new, I shall try to use the same psychoanalytic methods as we use in the treatment of our patients.*[350]

Considering that this is a text from 1969, it is doubtful that her approach can be regarded as new. Freud and several of his disciples had written extensively about myths with a very psychoanalytical perspective, indeed, not far from that used in their therapies.

Not to mention Jung — but he is not mentioned at all in Deutsch's book, although the Jungian mythologist Joseph Campbell is, as well as Károly Kerényi, together with whom Jung wrote a book in 1942 on mythology where Dionysus is

---

[348] Helene Deutsch, *A Psychoanalytic Study of the Myth of Dionysus and Apollo: Two Variants of the Son-Mother Relationship*, New York 1969, pp. 10f.

[349] Ibid., p. 13.

[350] Ibid., p. 15.

discussed at length.³⁵¹ It must have ben her loyalty to Freud that made her shun from even mentioning the foremost disciple of his to desert him. But it is an omission that casts doubts on her scientific honesty.

Dionysus is a complicated mythological figure already by having alternative versions even regarding his birth and lineage. Deutsch combines a couple of them, seeing those as describing different aspects of the story, i.e., of its psychological meaning.

At the core of the Dionysian myths, she finds two topics, "Dionysus's bisexuality and his struggle for immortality."³⁵² There is also his relation to his mother playing a role in both those topics, mainly by being absent during his childhood and because she was a mere human, which would make him less of a god. Here, Deutsch uses the version of the myth where the mother is Semele. The father, in just about all versions, is Zeus.

As for his bisexuality, Deutsch finds it indicated by "his not always masculine behavior," which in turn was caused by his childhood "lacking in objects for masculine identification."³⁵³ His personal struggle, then, is one between his masculinity and femininity.

This is a strange and outdated view on bisexuality. It is not the result of femininity in men, or for that matter masculinity in women. That doesn't even make any sense. Such a line of reasoning would instead lead to the equally fallacious idea of homosexuality caused by femininity in men and masculinity in women. Also, what is that femininity and masculinity really? There are no character traits being exclusively female or male. Those are just stereotypes that fall apart upon closer examination.

---

[351] Carl G. Jung & Károly Kerényi, *On a Science of Mythology: The Myth of the Divine Child and the Mysteries of Eleusis*, transl. R. F. C. Hull, New York 1949 (originally published in 1942).

[352] Deutsch 1969, p. 16.

[353] Ibid., p. 18.

Bisexuality is the attraction towards both genders, and it is proven to exist among both "female" and "male" personalities, as also Greek mythology tells us. Zeus was by all stereotype standards exceptionally "male" but still bisexual, which Deutsch herself mentions in the following chapter about Apollo.[354] So were several other deities. That was not an issue in Ancient Greece, which is frequently made clear in the writing of Plato.

It was more of a sensitive issue in Deutsch's days, but she could hardly claim to make sense of ancient mythology by applying modern conventions and prejudice to it. That would certainly trigger the wrath of Zeus.

Still, she goes so far as to interpret the outcome of the story, with Dionysus bringing his mother to Olympus:

The victory of Dionysus's masculinity over his femininity was necessary for, and has made possible, the unification of mother and son — and thus, at last, as god and goddess![355]

Deutsch was far from alone among the psychoanalysts of her days to foster these strange ideas about masculinity, femininity, and sexuality. Heterosexuality and fixed gender roles were regarded as healthy conditions, and deviations from these norms were seen as neurotic. When applied to the Greek myths, these views could but lead astray.

Apollo Killing Mothers
About Apollo, too, there are many myths describing his background and activities differently, and Helene Deutsch uses bits and pieces from several of them. She explains that it is not her goal to compare these versions and estimate their validity, but:

---

[354] Ibid., p. 77.
[355] Ibid., p. 43.

> *I wish, rather, to follow the psychological paths of Apollo's mythical life, to arrive at a plausible unification of these paths, by applying the analytic method of interpretation, where there is sufficient material.*[356]

She adds in a footnote that she found Pindar's *Odes* the most valuable of the sources, "because his writings are true to the purely mythical character of Apollo." It is unclear what she means by that. The sun god is certainly mythical since he cannot be confirmed as a historical figure, but any account of him would make that obvious.

In her view, Apollo nourished hostility towards women, especially mothers, and had several of them killed. Not his own mother, though. Deutsch sees this as a process in which a darker, pre-Homeric period ruled by female deities connected to earth were conquered by the male rulers of heaven. Apollo played the major role in this, and he won a lot by it: "Apollo's mythological status as sun-god was achieved through matricidal acts against earth-goddesses"[357]

That description of primeval events in Greek mythology can certainly be discussed. Interestingly, though, she does not see this change of rulership as negative. She calls these earth-goddesses the dark rulers of the world and representatives of death, and paints a discouraging picture of the world before Apollo's conquest:

> *It must have been a dark, cold and gloomy world! Apollo came to conquer this world and to wrest the rule from women to grant it to men, to change matriarchy to patriarchy, darkness to light.*[358]

But it was not any altruistic wish for a better world that

---

[356] Ibid., p. 50.
[357] Ibid., pp. 51f.
[358] Ibid., p. 65.

led Apollo to the killing of mothers. Deutsch presents several reasons. One was his overwhelming anxiety of motherhood as such, because of its mystery and hence danger to men.[359] Another was that women's constant presence beside Zeus stole his attention from Apollo, whose love for his father was the center of his life.[360] Fundamentally, though, "the unconscious elements of Apollo's psyche have their roots in the mythical past in which mothers ruled."[361]

As with Dionysus, Deutsch discusses the bisexuality of Apollo, but sees that of the former as within himself and manifested by projection, whereas that of Apollo is more complicated: "He is psychologically androgynous, both homosexual and heterosexual." She does not expand on what that might mean, but calls his love "mostly narcissistic; he loves men like himself."[362]

The narcissism is not hard to spot. It is a prominent characteristic of any deity, regardless of gender, maybe even unavoidable because of their elevated status and superhuman powers. Just by them acknowledging their own grandeur, they can be described as narcissistic.

But Deutsch links it to homosexuality,[363] as if homosexual love would be a covert kind of self-love. That is highly doubtful, especially since narcissistic behavior is found among heterosexuals as well.

Calling Apollo both homo- and heterosexual is a strange way of using those labels. What can it mean other than bisexuality? Deutsch regards Apollo's sexuality as androgynous, as if he needed to be part male to love women, and part female to love men. This link between sexual preferences and gender

---

[359] Ibid., p. 82.
[360] Ibid., p. 76.
[361] Ibid., p. 66.
[362] Ibid., p. 71.
[363] Ibid., p. 72.

identity is common among psychoanalysts, but it remains to be proven. It seems to be firmly rooted in the Freudian — and Jungian — paradigm that anything but heterosexuality is some kind of dysfunction.

Regarding both Apollo and Dionysus, Helene Deutsch makes a number of claims that in their lack of arguments are little more than opinions. She interprets characters and their actions quite freely, and draws conclusions from those interpretations. That would still be fine, if those interpretations and conclusions were reasonable. But they are full of contradictions and far-fetched assumptions, mostly because of her obvious prejudice about gender as well as sexuality. She even calls bi-sexuality an eternal problem of mankind.[364]

It would be more adequate to call it an eternal problem of psychoanalysis.

---

[364] Ibid., p. 71.

Erich Fromm

Erich Fromm (1900-1980) was born in Germany to Jewish parents. He studied sociology and later psychoanalysis, opening a clinic in 1927. As the Nazi party got into power, he moved to USA in 1934, and stayed there for the remainder of his life. He never met Sigmund Freud, nor is any correspondence between them known.

His understanding of psychology was at first admittedly Freudian, but later deviated from Freud's principles on certain aspects. His main perspective was social psychology, although to him — and as he understood it, to Freud — it would be impossible to separate it from individual psychology. He stated in 1930, while still faithful to the Freudian perspective:

> *Freud emphasized that there is no individual psychology of man isolated from his social environment, because an isolated man does not exist.*[365]

As can be seen in the following, Fromm wrote extensively and repeatedly about religion, almost exclusively referring to the Bible and Christianity. His ideas about myths and fairy tales are presented in the book *The Forgotten Language*, which is also discussed here.

The Dogma of Christ

Fromm was already in 1930 inclined towards the social perspective, if not outright sociological. Nor did he shun from the political dynamics in society. This is evident in the essay from that year quoted above, *The Dogma of Christ*, where Fromm ex-

---

[365] Erich Fromm, *The Dogma of Christ, and Other Essays on Religion, Psychology, and Culture*, Greenwich Connecticut 1963, p. 15. The German original of the essay "The Dogma of Christ" is from 1930, translated by James Luther Adams. Fromm intentionally left it unchanged in the 1963 publication.

plained what he saw as a change of Christian dogma during its first few centuries, in interaction with social changes.

In his foreword to the 1963 edition, Fromm confesses to some hesitation about republishing the old text. "First of all, it was written in a period when I was a strict Freudian."[366] That was to change later on, although his respect for Freud and some of his theories remained. Still, Fromm was convinced by others to have the text republished, and he found that "the method of the application of psychoanalysis to historical phenomena is the one which has been developed in my subsequent books."[367]

The theme of the essay, the interaction between Christian dogma and social change, may seem rather far from psychology, but Fromm is examining "the extent to which the change in certain religious ideas is an expression of the psychic change of the people involved and the extent to which these changes are conditioned by their conditions of life."[368] To Fromm, these two aspects are inseparable. He is convinced of the major role of the unconscious in this process:

The evolution of dogma can be understood only through knowledge of the unconscious, upon which external reality works and which determines the content of consciousness.

Fromm, not unlike Freud, explains God as a transference of childish emotions towards the parents "to a fantasy figure, to God."[369] And here, most definitely, the Freudian psychologist speaks: "In the adult's attitude toward God, one sees repeated the infantile attitude of the child toward his father."[370]

---

[366] Ibid., p. 11.
[367] Ibid., pp. 12f.
[368] Ibid., pp. 20f.
[369] Ibid., p. 25.
[370] Ibid., p. 27.

But then the socio-political perspective enters. Religion has the task of bringing people into the socially necessary infantile docility toward the authorities.[371] Therefore, God is always the ally of the rulers. A little later in the essay, Fromm expands on the role of religion:

Religion has a threefold function: for all mankind, consolation for the privations exacted by life; for the great majority of men, encouragement to accept emotionally their class situation; and for the dominant minority, relief from guilt feelings caused by the suffering of those whom they oppress.[372]

The first generations of Christians were mainly suppressed people of the lower classes: "They were the masses of the uneducated poor, the proletariat of Jerusalem, and the peasants in the country."[373] So, like John the Baptist, the early Christian doctrine addressed itself "not to the educated and the property owners, but to the poor, the oppressed, and the suffering."[374]

The early Christian community was loosely organized without any rigid hierarchy, "a free brotherhood of the poor, unconcerned with institutions and formulas."[375] Accordingly, the Jesus to whom they confessed their faith had like them been a regular human, who was adopted by God. Jesus was not the son of God to begin with, "but became so only by a definite, very distinct act of God's will."[376]

Although this needed God's active will, Fromm sees it as

---

[371] Ibid., p. 26.

[372] Ibid., p. 30.

[373] Ibid., p. 42.

[374] Ibid., pp. 43f.

[375] Ibid., p. 48.

[376] Ibid., p. 50.

a rebellion against the father-god. He suddenly had a co-regent. That indicated a wish for a complete replacement:

> *The belief in the elevation of a man to god was thus the expression of an unconscious wish for the removal of the divine father.*[377]

To confirm this early Christian belief, Fromm mentions *Psalms* 2:7, where God says: "You are my son, today I have begotten you," which is quoted in *Acts* 13:33, where it is applied to Jesus. Still, Fromm admits to at least one important exception in early Christianity: "But to Paul, Jesus was the Son of God from the very beginning."

Psychologically speaking, this Christianity was filled with aversion against the authorities — including the highest of them all, their god. When Jesus rose to his side, it was almost a rebellion. A man became a god, thereby challenging the existent one.

The early Christians believed that the misfortune of their lives would be reversed at the second coming, which they regarded as imminent: "The core of the missionary preaching of the early communion was, 'The kingdom of God is at hand.'"[378] That would also be the day when their oppressors would be punished. Fromm refers to *Luke* 6:20-25, where Jesus promises that the poor and the hungry are blessed and will be compensated, whereas the opposite shall happen to the rich and full.

This sympathy with the people at the bottom of the hierarchy and antipathy towards the ones at the top explains "the enormous influence which the teaching about the crucified and suffering savior immediately had upon the Jewish masses, and soon upon the pagan masses as well."[379]

But here Fromm might have gotten carried away. There

---

[377] Ibid., p. 54.
[378] Ibid., p. 62.
[379] Ibid., p. 52.

was not much of an influence on the Jewish masses, and the pagans took some time convincing. Through the 1st century, Christians were hardly more than a nuisance in Rome. Their worship was even a crime until the beginning of the 4th century. Were it not for the gradual acceptance of the religion in the ruling classes, Christianity might have remained little more than a cult that eventually faded away.

But during the first couple of centuries after its introduction in Rome, the upper classes increasingly adopted Christianity, until even the Roman emperor Constantine did so, decriminalizing it in the year 313. In 380 Christianity was declared the state religion.[380]

The success came at a price. In that long process towards recognition and government acceptance, the Christian dogma transformed to primarily fit the ruling class. Although the change was in the dogma, the reason for it was social: "The theological change is the expression of a sociological one, that is, the change in the social function of Christianity."[381]

The revised dogma was fixed by the Nicene Creed in a lengthy process during the fourth century. Fromm describes it as a fundamental transformation of Christianity from the religion of the oppressed to the religion of the rulers and of the masses manipulated by them.[382] He goes on:

> *Christianity, which had been the religion of a community of equal brothers, without hierarchy or bureaucracy, became the "church," the reflected image of the absolute monarchy of the Roman Empire.*

A strictly organized church was the consequence of this, as was the idea that now, salvation was made accessible

---

[380] Fromm mistakenly claims that Christianity became the state religion under Constantine. Ibid., p. 60.

[381] Ibid., p. 69.

[382] Ibid., p. 65.

through the church instead of simply through the trust in Jesus and the following of his commands. The church became holy, and became an intermediary between the Christians and their god:

> *Originally it was not the church but God alone who could forgive sins. Later,* Extra ecclesiam nulla salus;[383] *the church alone offers protection against any loss of grace.*[384]

The bitter irony of it was that "the priests granted pardon and expiation for the guilt feeling which they themselves had engendered."[385]

The most important change was in how Jesus was viewed. He was no longer regarded as adopted by God, but his son, a part of him, present since before the dawn of creation. It made all the difference in the world: "A man was not elevated to a god, but a god descended to become a man."[386] Jesus was no longer ever really human — he just walked the earth for a few years in the disguise of one.

In reality, according to this new doctrine, he was of one nature with the heavenly father. Fromm emphasizes it with italics: *"The decisive element was the change from the idea of man becoming God to that of God becoming man."*[387]

Thereby, the rebellion against the highest authority was gone, since God now was regarded as identical with Jesus. The hostility towards the father and the Oedipus crime it implied were gone. Authority was again revered.

For the people in the shadows of the castles and the churches, the victims of the new dogma, there was still one

---

[383] "Outside the Church there is no salvation."

[384] Ibid., p. 66.

[385] Ibid., p. 71.

[386] Ibid., p. 66.

[387] Ibid., p. 67.

comfort, although illusionary: "The masses found their satisfaction in the fact that their representative, the crucified Jesus, was elevated in status, becoming himself a pre-existent God."[388] And instead of hoping for the reckoning of a second coming, the people settled for being satisfied in the fantasy of a blissful hereafter.[389]

Fromm finds this development inevitable. The masses had little or no chance against the establishment. The authorities, all the way up to the god, were immovable. What was left for the people was to accept the situation:

> *It was hopeless to overthrow the father, then the better psychic escape was to submit to him, to love him, and to receive love from him. This change of psychic attitude was the inevitable result of the final defeat of the oppressed class.*[390]

The real winners were, of course, the high and mighty. When previously the blame was with the oppressors, each person was now personally responsible for any shortcomings and in need of relief from the sense of guilt. Everyone was a sinner:

> *No longer were the rulers to blame for wretchedness and suffering; rather, the sufferers themselves were guilty. They must reproach themselves if they are unhappy.*[391]

Since suffering was now the grace of God, with the model of Jesus, the rulers were innocent: "It relieved them of the guilt feelings they experienced because of the distress and suffering of the masses whom they had oppressed and exploited."[392]

---

[388] Ibid., p. 68.
[389] Ibid., pp. 71f.
[390] Ibid., p. 69.
[391] Ibid., p. 70.
[392] Ibid., p. 71.

The model with the son and the father being one from the beginning did create a logical problem, actually a contradiction. How could the father and the son be identical? In order to convince the believers, Fromm states that the doctrine had to have a specific, unconscious meaning. And he finds one: "There is one actual situation in which this formula makes sense, the situation of the child in its mother's womb."[393] They are two, yet one. That demanded quite a metamorphosis, leading to a very different deity: "The strong, powerful father has become the sheltering and protecting mother."

Eventually, that also led to the Mary cult, the increased Catholic focus on the mother of Jesus, which would in a way make her the mother of the god who created her — another paradox. But Fromm is not interested in this paradox. He refers to the mother cult as such, the transformation of the god as a father-figure to one with the traits of a mother-figure. And it makes the psychoanalyst in him wake up:

> *The full significance of the collective fantasy of the nursing Madonna becomes clear only through the results of psychoanalytic clinical investigations.*[394]

He does not expand on the subject, but finds another consequence: "This meant also that men had to regress to a passive, infantile attitude."[395]

The process, then, from a father-god with an adopted son to more of a mother-god being one with the son, as if pregnant with him, had some psychological implications for the believers:

> *Described psychologically, the change taking place here is the change from an attitude hostile to the father, to an atti-*

---

[393] Ibid., p. 72.
[394] Ibid., p. 74.
[395] Ibid., p. 75.

tude passively and masochistically docile, and finally to that of the infant loved by its mother. If this development took place in an individual, it would indicate a psychic illness.[396]

But in the case of the Christian population, the reality was different because the situation was. Instead of the symptom of a psychic illness, it was a question of adaption: "It is an expression not of pathological disturbance but, rather, of adjustment to the given social situation."

Still, this is no ideal situation, since it renders people passive and helpless against the powers that rule them. Fromm finds hope in the emergence and continued presence of Protestantism, which does not have the same dogmatic trap. He ends his text by praising the potential of Protestantism, which must mean that he dismisses Catholicism for going in the opposite direction:

Only Protestantism turned back to the father-god. It stands at the beginning of a social epoch that permits an active attitude on the part of the masses in contrast to the passively infantile attitude of the Middle Ages.[397]

The Trinity and Other Anomalies

Fromm's analysis is clear and worthy of thought, but there are gaps in it. Since he discusses at length the Father and the Son and their fusion in the Nicene Creed, it is strange that he completely omits the third part of the Trinity — the Holy Spirit. It was adopted later, but before the end of the 4th century, and it has remained in Christian dogma ever since.

Fromm mentions neither the Trinity nor the Holy Spirit (or Ghost) even once in his essay. One has to wonder why. An obvious possibility is that the Holy Spirit does not fit the

[396] Ibid., p. 92.
[397] Ibid., pp. 92f.

Freudian focus on the Oedipus complex, which has only the three roles of the father, the mother, and the son. Fromm's model needs to keep this tight cast.

Furthermore, Freud was not much for speculations about something as elusive as a spirit. That was more Jung's department, and by 1930 they were wide apart. At a time when Fromm confessed to have been a strict Freudian, he would avoid such a concept. But it weakens his discussion. It is too big an omission. By ignoring the Trinity, he has given up on explaining the anomaly of it. And it is not the only anomaly.

Fromm claims that the idea of Jesus adopted by God is a kind of revolt against the latter. That is hard to fathom. An all-seeing god would not willingly invite a rebel to the highest position imaginable — the one right next to him. And where was there a sign of animosity towards God? Certainly not from Jesus, in anything he said according to the Gospels, nor from his disciples or from Paul in any of his letters.

The mere idea of rebellion against God would make people in that era horrified — or burst out laughing. God was the creator of the world, the ultimate power since forever. That was not questioned. There was no revolting against him. The trouble lay in understanding him and his will. Opposing it was out of the question.

There were lots of rebellions, the Bible as well as other sources tell us, but they were against the Romans or against Jewish rulers. Humans saw other humans as the main causes of their suffering or discontent. There is a lot of historical evidence for that. It is much harder to find indications of Fromm's claim that there would instead be discontent aimed at God.

Job of the Old Testament would be an example of someone blaming God for his misfortune — and not without cause. That was what Jung wrote a substantial text about, but several years after 1930, when Fromm's essay was originally written. And the *Book of Job* ends with God laboriously explaining that Job simply has no right to question the actions of his God. Only someone just as elevated and powerful could.

No, people of that era would hardly even unconsciously foster the idea of a rebellion against God. It would be like trying to alter the very fabric of the cosmos.

Actually, one might just as well say that the introduction of the principle of the Trinity was an action to diminish God, to divide his omnipotence. If Jesus was not adopted, but identical to God and still somehow separate, then God was no longer the sole ultimate. Add to that the Holy Spirit, and God is more like a team member than the sole sovereign. It does not matter that it was called a *homoousios*, a single essence. A god that can in some way be divided is divided.

According to the Gospels, Jesus repeatedly called himself "the son of man," which deviates from the Old Testament use of the indefinite form "son of man" as a way of expressing that someone is human and nothing more. While the meaning of the definite form is unclear among scholars to this day, it is hardly an argument for homoousios.

It is at least equally credible to claim that the Nicene Creed rebelled against the sovereignty of God as that the idea of adoptionism did. One thing is sure — the Christian church needed to define their god as something other than the god of the Jews. For that, it was not enough with Jesus as a prophet, not even as an adopted son of God. He needed to be God for the Christian church to have its own religion.

There is also something odd about the differences and consequences Fromm sees with a father-god versus a mother-god. One leads to optimistic and rebellious men, the other to masochistically docile infants. Why?

Again, the reverse is just as plausible. A dominant father-god could lead to submissive and scared humans, whereas a protective mother-god would fill them with confidence and self-worth, thereby fostering a strong stance against injustice to them.

Freud was not famous for gender equality. The way he dismissed the possibility of an Electra complex as a female counterpart to the Oedipus one is a tell-tale, and there are many more in his writing. Fromm might here have been prejudiced by that flaw in Freudian thinking.

What is undeniable, though, is Fromm's claim that by time Christianity developed a hierarchy, a church which soon became part of the oppression. The first generations of Christians in Jerusalem and in the catacombs of Rome could hardly have imagined that. It would seem nightmarish to them — probably to Jesus as well, considering his outspoken contempt for the priests of Jerusalem.

Fromm implies that this change came from above in the hierarchy. As the upper classes joined the movement they adapted it to their preferences, and the lower classes were unable to resist. He suggests that the latter were not even aware of the gradual change. That can be discussed.

Normally when a movement grows, its administration does, too, and its structure tends to become more rigid. Mostly it can be explained as the price of success, like the successful businessman having to spend more and more time with his accountants. There is not necessarily an initial evil intent in that. But of course, when a movement forms into a hierarchy, those on top and those at the bottom will live under very different circumstances. Usually, the top doesn't seem to mind.

The question is to what extent it was planned. As noted by Bishop François de Sales in 1604: "Hell is full of good wills or desires."[398]

Escape from Freedom

In 1941, eleven years after the above essay, Erich Fromm treated another biblical subject — that of the expulsion of Adam and Eve from Eden. He did so in *Escape from Freedom*, which may be his most widely recognized book. It was meant

---

[398] "L'enfer est plein de bonnes volontés ou désirs." In a letter to Madame de Chantal dated November 21, 1604, he attributed the proverb to Bernard of Clairvaux. Saint François de Sales, *Œuvres complètes: Lettres*, volume 1, Paris 1821, p. 411.

to be part of a bigger project, but he decided to break his schedule to get this one out swiftly. His reason was the ongoing war and the dark forces instigating it. He wrote in the foreword:

> *Present political developments and the dangers which they imply for the greatest achievements of modern culture — individuality and uniqueness of personality — made me decide to interrupt the work on the larger study and concentrate on one aspect of it which is crucial for the cultural and social crisis of our day: the meaning of freedom for modern man.*[399]

He was saddened and alarmed at this outbreak of totalitarianism: "We have been compelled to recognize that millions in Germany were as eager to surrender their freedom as their fathers were to fight for it."[400] But it was not only Germany and Italy. He saw signs of the same threat in other European nations. And he sought to explain it in terms of social psychology, which he believed was necessary in order to defeat the enemy: "For, the understanding of the reasons for the totalitarian flight from freedom is a premise for any action which aims at the victory over the totalitarian forces."[401]

By this time, he had admittedly moved far from his initially strict Freudian views, in particular regarding the importance of the social dynamics in society:

> *The viewpoint presented in this book differs from Freud's inasmuch as it emphatically disagrees with his interpretation of history as the result of psychological forces that in themselves are not socially conditioned.*[402]

---

[399] Erich Fromm, *Escape from Freedom* (*Die Furcht vor der Freiheit*, 1941), New York 1976 (1st edition in English 1941), p. vii.

[400] Ibid., p. 5.

[401] Ibid., p. viii.

[402] Ibid., p. 14.

Fromm examines the emergence of human freedom from the boundaries of nature that surrounds him, as well as from just identifying with the collective of the human species. This realization was what truly initiated the development of human society:

> *The social history of man started with his emerging from a state of oneness with the natural world to an awareness of himself as an entity separate from surrounding nature and men.*[403]

Interestingly, this process of the individual separation from the surrounding world Fromm calls *individuation*, a term otherwise made famous by Jung. While to Jung it is an introspective discovery, Fromm sees it as basically extrovert. It is man finding his identity different from nature, at first, and then also from fellow men. Fromm regards it as having reached its peak in the centuries between the Reformation and the present.

As a representation of this process and its complications, he turns to the biblical myth of the expulsion of Adam and Eve from the Garden of Eden. He has a fresh and radical take on the meaning of the story, quite different from the biblical one:

> *The myth identifies the beginning of human history with an act of choice, but it puts all emphasis on the sinfulness of this first act of freedom and the suffering resulting from it.*[404]

When Adam and Eve take their bites of the forbidden fruit they may commit a sin in the eyes of God, but they do suddenly break free of the spell of Eden and make up their own

[403] Ibid., p. 24.
[404] Ibid., pp. 33f.

minds. They become separate from both God and the rest of his creation. In doing so, they achieve knowledge of good and bad, no less.

Thereby, they take the first step towards the ability to make up their own minds: "The act of disobedience as an act of freedom is the beginning of reason."

To Fromm, this first act of freedom is the first *human* act. Man has become separate from nature and has thereby taken the first step towards becoming an individual.

> *He acts against God's command, he breaks through the state of harmony with nature of which he is a part without transcending it. From the standpoint of the church which represented authority, this is essentially sin. From the standpoint of man, however, this is the beginning of human freedom.*

This is far from an ideal state, though. By breaking free, man has also lost something: "He is alone and free, yet powerless and afraid." There was security in the care of God and life in Eden, and there was carelessness in ignorance.

Fromm describes it as the crucial difference between "freedom from" and "freedom to."[405] The former happens when the bonds are broken, but then the latter is needed — a meaningful active entrance into freedom and all that it can bring of continued individuation, of finding one's own life. There is sweetness in the revelation of one's individuality, and once it has happened there is no turning back.

Yet, there is a catch in this new perception of oneself in the world:

> *But on the other hand this growing individuation means growing isolation, insecurity, and thereby growing doubt concerning one's own role in the universe, the meaning of*

---

[405] Ibid., p. 35.

one's life, and with all that a growing feeling of one's own powerlessness and insignificance as an individual.[406]

Fromm sees only one possible solution for how the individualized man should relate to this brand-new world. It is by "his active solidarity with all men and his spontaneous activity, love and work, which unite him again with the world, not by primary ties but as a free and independent individual."

For this to work, the social situation must allow it and make it possible. Society must be so structured that it encourages this process. If not — if the economic, social, and political conditions do not make it possible — freedom becomes an unbearable burden.

This is the sad case, Fromm concludes. The consequence is that although the full emergence of the individual has gone on since the Renaissance and seems to have come to a climax, "the lag between 'freedom from' and 'freedom to' has grown too."[407]

Judgment Is Reciprocal

Fromm uses this biblical tale to illustrate what he sees as a principal development in the psyche of humankind, which is the realization of an 'I' distinctive from everyone and everything else in the world. As it happened in the history of our evolution, similarly Fromm sees it happen in the growing infant.[408]

He does not insist that his interpretation of the biblical myth is the one also mythologically applicable, or at all intended by its ancient author. He merely uses it for his argument.

But the expulsion from Eden has mythological significance and similar accounts are found in other creation stories. In quite a number of them, humankind is regarded by the dei-

---

[406] Ibid., p. 36.
[407] Ibid., p. 37.
[408] Ibid., pp. 30f.

ties as something of a nuisance. We have no problem understanding why. This species is a difficult one to master or please. We only need to look at how hard it is for us to live peacefully among ourselves. Gods would do right to be wary of us.

The fall of man is part of the Bible's second creation story, and creation stories have their own rationale. Their main object is to explain in their own way what led to the present situation for humankind and the world — the present of the time of their composing, that is. They sort of filled in the blanks of human knowledge and understanding, and those were numerous in ancient times.

Accordingly, this particular biblical creation myth gives an account of why humans are mortal, why childbirth is painful, why snakes have no legs, and so on.

The most interesting part of this myth is indeed what fruit the first humans ate[409] — that of the tree which gives knowledge of good and bad. It implies that before Adam and Eve learned this, they were really neither good nor bad, since it would be impossible without knowledge of the concept. It really also makes them innocent of the crime of disobeying their god. They had no idea it would be bad.

It is an amusingly paradoxical situation, and God's reason for forbidding that fruit is not a noble one: It would make them more like him. He was already wary of his own creation, so he wanted to avoid the humans also eating of the tree of life, thereby becoming immortal like him. To stop that from happening, he had to expel them from Eden.

Still, it is food for thought that God would be so opposed to humans learning about good and bad, especially since he already in Eden expected them to act according to those principles. What was so dangerous about the ability to understand

---

[409] The biblical text does not specify the fruit. In European depiction it has long been an apple, probably because of the Latin *Versio Vulgata* of the Bible, where apple and evil are spelled the same: *malum*. Several other fruits have been suggested in Jewish and Christian discourse.

morality? And the first consequence of their enlightenment was to cover their nakedness. That is not much of a moral issue. It is little more than what we today would call a dress code. Yet, it was so important to God that he made sure to give Adam and Eve garments of skins before throwing them out of Eden.[410]

God's own moral standard, as it is presented in the Old Testament, can be questioned. It is hard to see that the expulsion of Adam and Eve was from a moral ground, whatever God claimed. It seems more like self-defense.

In any case, the punishment cannot be said to fit the crime — especially since it affected every following generation of humankind, though they were never near that fruit. God even admits to this basic principle of justice that only the one committing a crime can be punished for it. He states in *Ezekiel* that the son should not bear the iniquity of the father, nor the other way around.[411]

Maybe God's aversion to humans learning about good and bad was that then they might judge his actions. Job learned that God did not accept to be denounced or in any way have his actions measured by the creatures of his making.

It is safe to say that God was far from perfect, which is a trait he shared with numerous deities of other mythologies. Actually, it is hard to find even the suggestion of perfection among gods, especially outside monotheism. Christian theology has mostly insisted on it, though, but often from a philosophical standpoint — he would not be almighty if he were not perfect. The one is supposed to postulate the other.

In any case, Fromm's use of the myth makes sense as a symbolic account of humankind becoming a reasoning species. Good and bad might upon closer examination be very complicated concepts, indeed, but the ability to make a judgment, coming to a conclusion, is fundamental in reasoning.

---

[410] Genesis 3:21.

[411] Ezekiel 18:20.

To Fromm, though, the most important discovery separating modern man from his primeval ancestors is self-awareness — realizing that I am not you, nor anything else around me. But that is not as evident in the expulsion myth as is the awakening of reason. Eve even stated that she would eat of the fruit because she desired to become wise.[412] That suggests a preexisting self-awareness. And certainly, Adam and Eve had not been unaware of being separate from one another, as well as from God, the snake, and everything else in the Garden of Eden.

It might be proposed that Adam and Eve reached self-awareness when discovering each other's nudity. Indeed, the shame they showed fits with the emotional meaning of becoming self-aware as a moment of embarrassment caused by some flaw in one's behavior or features. But that is not much of a revelation.

There is one act of what can be called individuation of sorts taking place in Eden, right before the expulsion: Adam names his previously nameless wife Eve.[413] Although it is he who does it, and not she, it is still recognition of her own identity. Considering she was the one making them taste the fruit to receive its gift, she was worth it.

Psychoanalysis and Religion

Nine years after the above book, Erich Fromm published another one expressly on the theme of religion, *Psychoanalysis and Religion*. This was in 1950, a few years after the end of World War II, when Western materialism was blooming and the many comforts of modern industrialism got accessible to the populations of USA and Europe, initially, and soon to many countries around the world.

Fromm looked at this accelerating progress with ambiguity. A new horrific threat had appeared in that "scientists argue

---

[412] Genesis 3:6.
[413] Ibid., 3:20.

whether the atomic weapon will or will not lead to the destruction of the globe."[414] Although less dramatic, there was another threat to civilization, which may even have increased since then — the one of superficiality:

> *We have the most extraordinary possibilities for communication in print, radio, and television, and we are fed daily with nonsense which would be offensive to the intelligence of children were they not suckled on it.*[415]

Like so much of his writing, Fromm's treatment of religion from a psychoanalytical perspective is more of ethical and political agitation, almost comparable to a polemic pamphlet, than an academic treatise on the subjects of the title. He does describe religious attitudes and beliefs from a psychoanalytical standpoint, but with more words and vigor he argues for what religion should be and what role it should play in individual lives as well as in society. The personal take he allows himself is evident already in the foreword:

> *The views expressed in these chapters are in no sense representative of "psychoanalysis." There are psychoanalysts who are practicing religionists as well as others who consider the interest in religion a symptom of unsolved emotional conflicts. The position taken in this book differs from both and is, at most, representative of the thinking of a third group of psychoanalysts.*[416]

---

[414] Erich Fromm, *Psychoanalysis and Religion*, New Haven 1967 (1st edition 1950), p. 2. He made no changes in the 1967 edition, explaining in the foreword: "To my surprise I found that I felt no need for changes in essential points and have no objection to having the book printed again as it stands." Ibid., p. vi.

[415] Ibid., pp. 2f.

[416] Ibid., p. v.

In the book, he gives no indication of other members of that third group than himself. He is not even clear about his own beliefs, but they seem not to include a deity:

There need be no quarrel with those who retain the symbol God although it is questionable whether it is not a forced attempt to retain a symbol whose significance is essentially historical.[417]

Also, along the same line of reasoning:

The more man understands and masters nature the less he needs to use religion as a scientific explanation and as a magical device for controlling nature.[418]

Much like Jung, he complains that psychology has been reluctant to deal with spiritual content and its influence on the psyche. He sees this as a consequence of the discipline defining itself as a natural science: "Academic psychology, trying to imitate the natural sciences and laboratory methods of weighing and counting, dealt with everything except the soul."[419] But that changed with the work of Sigmund Freud, who is portrayed with superlatives:

Then came Freud, the last great representative of the rationalism of the Enlightenment, the first to demonstrate its limitations. He dared to interrupt the songs of triumph of mere intellect.

It leads Fromm to a conclusion he shares with Jung, which is that only two professional groups are concerned with the

---

[417] Ibid., p. 114.
[418] Ibid., p. 104.
[419] Ibid., p. 6.

soul: priests and psychoanalysts.[420] As for the latter he mentions Freud and Jung, citing two works that he leans on to present psychoanalytical thought on religion: *The Future of an Illusion* by Freud, which Fromm calls one of his most profound and brilliant books, and *Psychology and Religion* by Jung, "who was the first psychoanalyst to understand that myth and religious ideas are expressions of profound insights."[421]

Comparing the theories in those books, though, Fromm is quick to criticize Jung on several grounds, but not at all Freud. He opposes the understanding that Freud would be a foe of religion and Jung a friend of it. Instead, he concludes about their standpoints:

> *Freud opposes religion in the name of ethics — an attitude which can be termed "religious." On the other hand, Jung reduces religion to a psychological phenomenon and at the same time elevates the unconscious to a religious phenomenon.*[422]

It is doubtful that either of them would agree with this conclusion. Both Freud and Jung definitely related to religion primarily as a psychological phenomenon. Freud was an outspoken atheist, and said so clearly also in *The Future of an Illusion*. The illusion in the title is that of religious belief.

Jung stressed, like Fromm, the reality of religion in human minds regardless of the existence of any god. His idea of the collective unconscious, which must be what Fromm refers to, is definitely not one of divine character. He described it more like a highly developed inherited entity, comparable to the instincts although of much greater complexity. Jung was always vague about his own religious beliefs, but clear about them having no bearing on his theories.

---

[420] Ibid., p. 7.
[421] Ibid., p. 10.
[422] Ibid., p. 20.

Fromm presents his own definition of religion: "I understand by religion *any system of thought and action shared by a group which gives the individual a frame of orientation and an object of devotion.*"[423]

This definition is both wide and vague. It would fit patriots of any nation, members of a political party, the fans of a rock group, and the supporters of a football team. Actually, it would fit just about any subculture. Both "frame of orientation" and "devotion" are insufficiently precise to have any meaning in a definition.

Certainly, there is no fixed definition of religion on which scholars completely agree, but the component of the supernatural and the belief in laws other than those of nature ruling existence are usually included. One might say that religion has elements that are by their nature impossible to prove in the physical world, and therefore need to be a matter of faith.

But that is exactly what Fromm wants to avoid. He argues for widening the concept of religion to practices and traditions without deities and other elements of pure faith, in order to incorporate ethical and philosophical teachings that would otherwise be hard to include. It becomes clear when he presents a division of religions into *authoritarian* and *humanistic*.[424]

Authoritarian religion is the one with a church deciding the dogma and people are to submit to deities like sheep to the shepherd. Fromm finds an interesting correlation between the deity and humankind: "The more perfect God becomes, the more imperfect becomes man."[425] The elevated deity demands obedience and gives room for little else. Humans are supposed to lower their heads in shame afore the deity.

In humanistic religion, people are free, even expected, to take care of their own spiritual development: "Man must develop his power of reason in order to understand himself, his

---

[423] Ibid., p. 21. The italics are Fromm's.
[424] Ibid., p. 34.
[425] Ibid., p. 50.

relationship to his fellow men and his position in the universe."[426]

Fromm uses the analogy of the fall and the flood of the Bible.[427] The former, where Adam and Eve are expelled from Eden for breaking God's command, is authoritarian. But in the story of the flood, Noah is working together with God to survive the flood, and after it there is the covenant between God and Noah, where both have obligations. That, to Fromm, is a sign of a humanistic religion.

He finds humanistic religion in parts of otherwise authoritarian dogma, as well as way outside that territory:

> *Illustrations of humanistic religions are early Buddhism, Taoism, the teachings of Isaiah, Jesus, Socrates, Spinoza, certain trends in the Jewish and Christian religions (particularly mysticism), the religion of Reason of the French Revolution.*[428]

That is a wide scope. It is particularly odd to find Socrates and Spinoza there, who are otherwise referred to as philosophers.

Taoism, too, is more readily explained as a philosophy than as a religion. It might even be said about early Buddhism, and probably also for the *Culte de la Raison* of the French Revolution, which intended to replace Christianity with atheistic devotion towards the ideals of liberty, equality, and fraternity.

Fromm has widened the definition so much to incorporate this diversity, he might as well have gone the other way and found a concept in which to include religion.

If so, the concept would not be philosophy, which is also wide and vague to say the least. But moral philosophy or ethics seem accurate for what Fromm discusses. The ideology of it

---

[426] Ibid., p. 37.
[427] Ibid., pp. 42ff.
[428] Ibid., p. 37.

stands out when he describes the true follower of humanistic religion, which is certainly what he advocates:

> *He must develop his powers of love for others as well as for himself and experience the solidarity of all living beings.*[429]

Love is an ideal that Fromm stresses repeatedly as being at the core of his favorite form of religion:

> *The command to 'Love thy neighbor as thyself!' is, with only slight variations in its expression, the basic principle common to all humanistic religions.*[430]

He even makes it the optimal goal of psychoanalysis, writing in italics: "*Analytic therapy is essentially an attempt to help the patient gain or regain his capacity for love.*"[431] He seems to think that without the component of love — and that of truth, something even Pontius Pilate knew the need to elaborate upon — there is not much for psychoanalysis to bother about:

> *The psychoanalyst is in a position to study the human reality behind religion as well as behind nonreligious symbol systems. He finds that the question is not whether man returns to religion and believes in God but whether he lives love and thinks truth. If he does so the symbol systems he uses are of secondary importance. If he does not they are of no importance.*[432]

Though love is in just as dire need of a definition as religion (and truth), Fromm makes no effort at it. It is a pity, since there is a fountain of thoughts on the subject in both philoso-

---

[429] Ibid.
[430] Ibid., p. 86.
[431] Ibid., p. 87.
[432] Ibid., p. 9.

phy and religion, such as the Greek distinctions between *eros*, *agape*, and *philia*, also discussed for many centuries in Christian theology. Fromm with his take on psychoanalysis should have a go, too.

Without doing so, he risks falling into the trap of contributing to the "nonsense which would be offensive to the intelligence of children" he warns about. We all know that we should love one another, but even when we do so it often turns out much more complicated than what was foreseen. Love is no fix-all magic potion, and when it is, as in the story of Tristan and Iseult, it ends with disaster.

Fromm must have some theory about the nature of love, since he states that "psychoanalysis also shows that love by its very nature cannot be restricted to one person."[433] He does not refer to self-love, but to loving just one other person. So, the love he speaks about might be compassion.

While neglecting to define love with his psychoanalytical tools, Fromm applies them to the inspired sense of oneness that is a common religious experience, such as in the ecstasy of some devoted Catholics and the experience of *satori* in Zen meditation:

> *It is this process of breaking through the confines of one's organized self — the ego — and of getting in touch with the excluded and disassociated part of oneself, the unconscious, which is closely related to the religious experience of breaking down individuation and feeling one with the All.*[434]

He adds that his use of the concept of the unconscious here is neither quite that of Freud nor that of Jung. His own definition of the unconscious — again being rather vague, if not circular — is "that part of our self which is excluded from

[433] Ibid., p. 87.
[434] Ibid., p. 96.

the organized ego which we identify with our self."[435] It contains "both the lowest and the highest, the worst and the best," which is not very clarifying. Still, it clearly deviates from both Freud's and Jung's ideas of the unconscious as something more orderly, with strictly defined functions.

There are no archetypes in Fromm's unconscious. He does not mention the term in his book. But he does express a similar understanding of the symbols that appear in myths as well as dreams:

> *Symbolic language is the only universal language the human race has known. It is the language used in myths five thousand years old and in the dreams of our contemporaries.*[436]

In this context, the universality of symbolic language, he makes no reference to Jung but he does mention Joseph Campbell's *The Hero with a Thousand Faces*, which is in turn inspired by Jung's thoughts. That cannot have been unknown to Fromm, who calls the book remarkable.[437]

Close to Jung

Reading Fromm, it is easy to come to the conclusion that his thoughts on psychoanalysis as well as his ethical agitation bring him much closer to Jung than to Freud. The same goes for his stance on religion and how psychoanalysis can approach it. His reluctance to compare Jung's ideas to his own may not stem so much from their differences as from a sense of competing on the very same arena.

One crucial element of psychoanalytical theory, where he outspokenly agrees more with Jung than with Freud, is that of the Oedipus complex. To Freud it was definitely an expression

---

[435] Ibid., p. 97.
[436] Ibid., p. 111.
[437] Ibid., p. 112, footnote.

of a longing for sexual incest at the root of the male psyche, but Jung found that interpretation far too narrow. He insisted that sexuality, though certainly important, is not that altogether dominant in the psyche and its complications. Often, he stated, it is a symbolic representation of something else.

Fromm has the same objection, and he even gives Jung credit:

> *Jung has pointed out the necessity of such revision of Freud's incest concepts clearly and convincingly in his early writings.*[438]

He says early writings, as if Jung would have changed his mind on this point. He did not.

Furthermore, Fromm suggests that Freud really had a nuanced view on the subject: "Freud himself has indicated that he means something beyond the sexual realm." A source on this would have been fine. I have not seen any sign of it in the writing of Freud that I have gone through.

Though Fromm praises Freud repeatedly and expresses ambivalence about Jung in his writing, the bulk of that writing shows more similarities to the latter than to the former. Fromm actually gives the impression of being a Jungian at heart, whatever he claims.

The Forgotten Language

Already the following year, in 1951, Fromm returned to the subject of mythology in *The Forgotten Language*, where he discussed the symbolism in dreams, myths, and fairy tales. He saw in all of them the same symbolic language, which he regarded as "the only universal language the human race ever developed."[439]

---

[438] Ibid., p. 82, footnote.

[439] Erich Fromm, *The Forgotten Language: An Introduction to the Understanding of Dreams, Fairy Tales and Myths*, New York 1951, p. vi.

He urged that its importance is such that it should be taught in schools just as other foreign languages.

His presentation of this symbolic language, though, is far from as structured and well-defined as is the rule for languages, and he readily admits to the many contradicting interpretations of it by his colleagues in psychoanalysis. Teaching it in high schools and colleges, as he suggests, would be a bumpy ride with the risk of confusing the students more than enlightening them.

Already his definition of this language makes it hard to handle with something similar to the precision of grammar and glossaries:

Symbolic language is a language in which inner experiences, feelings and thoughts are expressed as if they were sensory experiences, events in the outer world.[440]

That would make them akin to metaphors. The real world is used to explain and express inner sentiments:

Symbolic language is language in which the world outside is a symbol of the world inside, a symbol for our souls and our minds.[441]

Furthermore, he insists not only that this language is the same for dreams and myths, but also that it is the same for all cultures and throughout history.[442]

He divides these symbols into three kinds: conventional, accidental, and universal. Only the latter two contain symbolic language. The conventional symbols are the everyday ones we share and assign the same meaning, such as just about any noun in a language. The accidental ones are regular symbols

---

[440] Ibid., p. 7.
[441] Ibid., p. 12.
[442] Ibid., p. 7.

that have by personal experience been given a meaning not shared by others. The universal ones have a symbolic meaning shared by all. Fromm mentions fire and water as examples, in how they carry similar if not identical emotions and associations that go beyond their basic meanings.[443]

It is the language of the universal symbol that is "the one common tongue developed by the human race."[444] He explains this by its links to our traits as a species:

The universal symbol is rooted in the properties of our body, our senses, and our mind, which are common to all men and, therefore, not restricted to individuals or to specific groups.

This takes him very close to Jung's theory of the archetypes, which were also explained as universal because of their emergence from common human characteristics and experiences. Fromm even argues for the existence of these universal symbols in much the same way as Jung did for archetypes:

Evidence for this is to be found in the fact that symbolic language as it is employed in myths and dreams is found in all cultures in so-called primitive as well as such highly developed cultures as Egypt and Greece. Furthermore, the symbols used in these various cultures are strikingly similar since they all go back to the basic sensory as well as emotional experiences shared by men of all cultures.[445]

But Fromm never mentions the word archetype in his book, although he must have been familiar with it at this time, nor does he in any way compare Jung's theory to his.

He allows for some differences in meaning for symbols in

---

[443] Ibid., pp. 13ff.
[444] Ibid., p. 18.
[445] Ibid.

separate cultures and environments having separate natural conditions. He suggests that these variations can be compared to dialects. In addition, he allows for different experiences to alter the meanings and impressions of those symbols. Using again the example of fire, it can be both soothing against the cold and terrifying when a whole house is consumed in flames. Consequently, the interpretation of a symbol needs knowledge of the complete context:

> *The particular meaning of the symbol in any given place can only be determined from the whole context in which the symbol appears, and in terms of the predominant experiences of the person using the symbol.*[446]

No wonder he has trouble making a dictionary for this language.

Exploring these symbols and their meanings, Fromm mainly focuses on dreams, weighing heavily but not exclusively on Sigmund Freud's theories about dream interpretation. He claims that all dreams are meaningful and significant, always containing a significant message to the dreamer, because "we do not dream of anything that is trifling."[447]

Not that it makes interpreting dreams any more reliable than defining the language of symbols, since "the right interpretation depends on the state of mind that was predominant before the dreamer fell asleep."[448]

At the root of this mechanism of the psyche he finds the unconscious, but he points out that his definition of it deviates from those of Freud and Jung, using a different wording from that in *Psychoanalysis and Religion*, but also confusing:

> *It is neither Jung's mythical realm of racially inherited ex-*

---

[446] Ibid., p. 20.
[447] Ibid., p. 24.
[448] Ibid., p. 164.

perience nor Freud's seat of irrational libidinal forces. It must be understood in terms of the principle: "What we think and feel is influenced by what we do."[449]

Fromm's unconscious is simply another consciousness, not its secret ruler or guardian. It is the conscious of sleep as opposed to that of being awake, and never the twain shall meet since "the day world is as unconscious in our sleep experience as the night world is in our waking experience." Still, Fromm finds significant differences between the mind asleep and awake, making it seem like the former is superior to the latter, explaining in italics that *"we are not only less reasonable and less decent in our dreams but that we are also more intelligent, wiser, and capable of better judgment when we are asleep than when we are awake."*[450]

The capacity of the dream state is exemplified by the discovery of the formula of the benzene ring, which appeared in a dream.[451] What Fromm refers to is the German 19th century chemist August Kekulé, who had a dream of a snake biting its tail,[452] which made him realize the shape of the benzene molecule. Jung has also referred to it, with another version of the dream.[453]

But that dream revelation can be questioned. Kekulé described it: "I was sitting, writing at my text-book; but the work did not progress; my thoughts were elsewhere. I turned my chair to the fire and dozed." That's more of a daydream. He had made another dream revelation a few years earlier, which seems a bit much. He encouraged his students to dream, but

---

[449] Ibid., p. 29.

[450] Ibid., p. 33.

[451] Ibid., p. 45.

[452] The snake forming a circle by biting its tail is a symbol from antiquity called *ouroboros*.

[453] Carl G. Jung, *The Psychology of the Transference* (*Die Psychologie der Übertragung*, 1946), New York 1998, p. 4.

sensibly added, "let us beware of publishing our dreams before they have been put to the proof by the waking understanding."[454]

Jung and Fromm made more of it than Kekulé did.

Fromm's conception of the unconscious leads him to explain the meanings of dreams not so much by what the symbols stand for as by what functions the dreams have in the personal development of the dreamer.

He has the same approach to myths. His first example of how to recognize and understand symbolic language shows this clearly. It is the biblical story of Jonah, who was reluctant to heed God's command. Fromm claims that it is written in symbolic language and "all the realistic events described are symbols for the inner experiences of the hero."[455]

Thus, the ship's belly and that of the big fish are both examples of the isolated safety of the mother's womb, expressing Jonah's longing for it. When he realizes the imprisonment of it, he calls to God to let him out and then hurries to do his bidding.

The myth, Fromm explains, is a story just like the dream, but one that expresses, in symbolic language, religious and philosophical ideas.[456]

In his examples, though, neither religious nor philosophical issues are as prominent as those of personal psychology. Like with the dreams, he really describes myths as representations of individual emotional struggles.

This is a perspective he shares with Freud and Jung, although interpretations and conclusions about those struggles of the psyche may differ. For all three, the meaning of myths lies in the individual's internal complications and not in concepts of shared beliefs or theoretical speculations. In spite of

---

[454] John Read, *From Alchemy to Chemistry*, New York 1995 (1st edition 1957), 179f.

[455] Fromm, *The Forgotten Language*, p. 22.

[456] Ibid., p. 195.

the universality all three claim to find in the essence of myths, the message is always personal and not collective, psychological and not philosophical.

Thus, Fromm regards the Oedipus myth as one with the central theme of "the fundamental aspects of interpersonal relationships, the attitude toward authority."[457] That moves him far away from Freud's theory of the sexual Oedipus complex, but not from the interpretation of the myth as relating to the individual psyche and its internal struggles. When Oedipus kills his father, it is a rebellion of the son against the authority of the father, and wedding his mother he takes his father's place with all its privileges.[458]

Fromm goes on to describe the Oedipus myth as a symbolic tale of how once in the distant past a matriarchal culture was conquered by men and replaced with a patriarchal society. His source to this idea is the Swiss anthropologist and professor of Roman law Johann Jakob Bachofen (1815-1887), whose book *Das Mutterrecht* (*Mother Right*) from 1861 argued for the primeval existence of a matriarchy later replaced by a patriarchy. Fromm describes the differences between the two societies:

> *Matriarchal culture is characterized by an emphasis on ties of blood, ties to the soil, and a passive acceptance of all natural phenomena. Patriarchal society, in contrast, is characterized by respect for man-made law, by a predominance of rational thought, and by man's effort to change natural phenomena.*[459]

Fromm connects the three Sophocles plays referring to Oedipus — *King Oedipus, Oedipus at Colonus,* and *Antigone* — and states that they should be understood as "an attack against

---

[457] Ibid., p. 196.
[458] Ibid., p. 202.
[459] Ibid., p. 207.

the victorious patriarchal order by the representatives of the defeated matriarchal system."[460]

He sees the same conflict between matriarchy and patriarchy in the Babylonian creation myth *Enuma Elish*, which tells of a "victorious rebellion of male gods against Tiamat, the great mother who ruled the universe."[461] In this myth he also sees an expression of ancient male envy towards female ability to reproduce, which he regards as remaining to some extent:

> *Quite in contrast to Freud's assumption that the "penis envy" is a natural phenomenon in the constitution of the woman's psyche, there are good reasons for assuming that before male supremacy was established there was a "pregnancy envy" in the man, which even today can be found in numerous cases.*[462]

The male alternative in mythology — in *Enuma Elish* as well as in Genesis of the Bible — was creation by words, which is "to produce by the power of thought."[463]

Another example given of the battle of the sexes is the fairy tale *Little Red-Cap* (*Little Red Riding Hood*), which Fromm regards as a story of triumph by man-hating women.[464] The male inadequacy is shown by how the wolf "attempted to play the role of a pregnant woman, having living beings in his belly." Fromm sees the red cap worn by the girl of the story as a symbol of menstruation.[465]

He finishes his book by elaborately arguing for the main character of *The Trial* by Franz Kafka having a receptive orien-

---

[460] Ibid., p. 210.
[461] Ibid., p. 231.
[462] Ibid., p. 233.
[463] Ibid., p. 234.
[464] Ibid., p. 241.
[465] Ibid., p. 240.

tation: "All his strivings went in the direction of wanting to receive from others — never to give or to produce."[466] This is something the character does not realize until right before his execution, when he says: "I always wanted to snatch at the world with twenty hands, and not for a very laudable motive, either."[467]

Hypnopompic Dreams

The limited scope and the few examples of what Fromm calls a symbolic language do not suffice to give it even an introductory sketch of a structure. Compared to Jung's quite similar theory of the archetypes, it lacks the elaborate definitions and multitude of illustrative examples of the latter. It is more of a notion than a theory.

That shortcoming might be the result of his focus on dreams and his assumption that they are fully compatible with myths and tales. But dreams are elusive entities and at his own admission difficult to give universal meanings. They are creations of individual minds, and in a very unclear process at that. Even the recording of them is haphazard.

Fromm mentions that the content of a dream is very much dependent on the personal situation and emotions before sleep. As for the recording of them, though, another situation is unquestionably of much greater importance — the moment of waking up. Dreams cannot be recorded during sleep, so any retrieval of them needs to be done when awake — and very soon, since they are quickly dissolving.

The significant moments where dreams are accessible to the conscious mind are two: *hypnagogia*, when the mind moves from wakefulness to sleep, and *hypnopompia*, when it goes from sleep to wakefulness. In the former, it is possible for dreams to start taking shape according to a conscious will. Whether that is the case also for hypnopompic dreams is not as easy to as-

---

[466] Ibid., p. 251.
[467] Ibid., p. 262.

certain, but far from implausible. If that is the case, interpretations of dreams perceived when waking up must be done with the reservation that they might be formed at least partly by the conscious mind when waking up.

Although that would put the psychoanalysis of those dreams in a completely different light, the dilemma has — as far as I have found — been ignored not only by Fromm, but also by Freud and Jung. It is understandable, though indeed questionable, since it would risk making the unconscious unreachable by dream analysis in any reliable way.

The dreams retold by Fromm et al. are sometimes suspiciously extended and detailed. It is unlikely that they have been free of reconstruction and additions by the conscious mind. That is particularly the case when they have a long narrative where events follow events in an orderly and fully comprehensible fashion.

Dreams reconstructed in such a manner would actually make their formation closer to what can be assumed of myths — strange tales composed and transmitted by conscious minds. To understand the symbols in myths, searching their parallels in dreams would then be a detour. They should be possible to decipher as expressions of the conscious mind alone.

You Shall Be as Gods

In 1966, Fromm returned to the subject of religion and mythology in *You Shall Be as Gods: A Radical Interpretation of the Old Testament and Its Tradition*. There is not much of psychoanalysis in his text, which discusses the Old Testament mainly from a theological perspective. Nor is the interpretation strikingly radical.

Fromm claims not to be a theist[468] and calls his personal

---

[468] Erich Fromm, *You Shall Be as Gods: A Radical Interpretation of the Old Testament and Its Tradition*, Greenwich 1966, p. 10.

form of spirituality a nontheistic mysticism.[469] As for the deity, he states, "I believe that the concept of God was a historically conditioned expression of an inner experience." That does in no way stop him from holding the Old Testament in the highest regard:

> *The Old Testament is a* revolutionary *book; its theme is the liberation of man from the incestuous ties to blood and soil, from the submission to idols, from slavery, from powerful masters, to freedom for the individual, for the nation, and for all of mankind.*[470]

It is with this view he spends the just under 200 pages of the book explaining what he regards as the proper way to interpret the Bible, which is that of radical humanism:

> *By radical humanism I refer to a global philosophy which emphasizes the oneness of the human race, the capacity of man to develop his own powers and to arrive at inner harmony and at the establishment of a peaceful world.*[471]

It is quite an idealistic standpoint. He means that the god of the Old Testament promoted mankind's strife to achieve freedom — maybe even from the need of God.[472] Foremost in this struggle for freedom is discarding any kind of idol worship. To Fromm, idolatry is at the root of the unliberated and unrealized human being. It represents the object of man's central passion, "the desire to return to the soil-mother, the craving for possession, power, fame, and so forth."[473]

---

[469] Ibid., p. 18.
[470] Ibid., pp. 9f.
[471] Ibid., pp. 14f.
[472] Ibid., p. 23.
[473] Ibid., p. 36.

He also states:

The idol is the alienated form of man's experience of himself. In worshiping the idol, man worships himself.[474]

This is one of the few instances of a psychological perspective in the book. Another is when he sets out to define the so-called religious experience, which to him is the same whether theistic or nontheistic. Therefore, he relinquishes using the word religious for it, but calls it the *x experience*. He names five psychological aspects of it:

1. The experience of life as a question requiring an answer,
2. Setting the highest values for one's development,
3. Transforming to become more human,
4. Letting go of one's ego and fears,
5. Leaving selfishness and learning to love life.[475]

These aspects seem more ethical than psychological, but Fromm insists:

It follows from all the foregoing considerations that the analysis of the x experience moves from the level of theology to that of psychology and, especially, psychoanalysis.[476]

That is because it calls for an understanding of unconscious processes underlying the x experience. But it has to go beyond Freud's outline of psychoanalysis, focused almost exclusively on the libido:

---

[474] Ibid., p. 37.
[475] Ibid., pp. 47ff.
[476] Ibid., p. 49.

> *The central problem of man is not that of his libido; it is that of dichotomies inherent in his existence, his separateness, alienation, suffering, his fear of freedom, his wish for union, his capacity for hate and destruction, his capacity for love and union.*[477]

Instead, Fromm suggests an empirical psychological anthropology, studying such experiences regardless of conceptualizations.

As for humankind's quest for freedom, its realization is the true meaning of a messianic time to come. It is the next step in history and not at all a doomsday: "The messianic time is the time when man will have been fully born."[478] At that point humans are liberated to act according to their finest potentials. Also the Sabbath, the day when things are left as they are, is a symbol of this:

> *The Sabbath is the expression of the central idea of Judaism: the idea of freedom; the idea of complete harmony between man and nature, man and man; the idea of the anticipation of the messianic time and of man's defeat of time, sadness, and death.*[479]

Fromm's thoughts and sentiments are romantic, if not naïve, and his reasoning shows profound loyalty towards the Old Testament and the long Jewish tradition of its interpretation. It is all but completely within this scope that he goes to find support for his own interpretation. Therefore, it does not deviate significantly from that tradition.

His reverence sets him far apart from Freud's treatment of Moses as well as Jung's speculations based on the Book of Job. At no instance does he really question the wisdom of the Bible

---

[477] Ibid., p. 50.
[478] Ibid., p. 98.
[479] Ibid., p. 153.

or its god, although he states that he does not regard it as the words of God, but "historical examination shows that it is a book written by men — different kinds of men, living in different times." Still, he persistently discusses it in a tone of dealing with something sacred and unquestionable.

Also, he insists on treating the whole of the Hebrew Bible as one book, although it has been compiled from many sources. His argument is that through its long history it has become one book.[480]

It is a pity that he makes this choice, since it ignores the many different contextual settings and their clues to inconsistencies as well as intentions. By relating to the Old Testament as both unquestionable and timeless, there is not much of an analysis left for Fromm to do.

Therefore, his conclusion is not different from that of its believers, which is that the biblical god is set on showing humankind the way to bliss, and if we just understand and follow his commands we will get there.

That can be questioned, but Fromm definitely does not. The good faith of this nontheist sometimes clogs his reasoning, when he explains the rationale of God's behavior. For example, when discussing the terribly fearsome side of the almighty, Fromm makes a distinction between threat and prediction, where the latter is creating awareness of the consequences instead of simply scaring people to change their ways. He asks the following rhetorical question, which does not help his case:

> *Does a father, telling his son that he will spank him if he does not do his homework, threaten him or is his threat an indirect expression of the prediction that he will fail in school (and in life) if he does not acquire self-discipline and a sense of responsibility?*[481]

---

[480] Ibid., pp. 10f.
[481] Ibid., p. 139.

The simple answer is that yes, it is a threat and nothing else, whatever the intention. A prediction would be if the father warned him that he will get a failing grade if not doing his homework, but the punishment he threatens his son with has no direct relation to the consequences of the boy's studying efforts. It is a means of pressuring him to comply, in other words a threat.

The god of the Bible has indeed made the same kind of threats and on a much grander scale. People must obey or else, simply because he demands it. And the punishments he threatens with are usually monstrously out of proportion. No wonder the people of his creation, as well as the boy threatened with spanking, have great difficulty learning the lesson.

Fromm's reasoning in *You Shall Be as Gods* is similar, even repetitious, of his discussions in the above-mentioned books. It is clear that the psychologist in him has been drowned out by the ideologist. That may be commendable, but for the purpose of this book's topic it is disappointing. Although he writes extensively about religion, he contributes little to the psychoanalysis of mythology.

Shifting Perspectives

There is quite a change of perspectives between what Fromm wrote in the essay *The Dogma of Christ*, when he was 30 years old, and that in *You Shall Be as Gods*, when he was 66. In the former text he spoke about how Christianity developed into a tool of oppression of the masses, and he bluntly called God a fantasy figure. In the latter he speaks passionately about the potential blessing of what he sees as the true message of the Bible.

Of course, he speaks of two separate religions — Christianity versus Judaism — but it still reveals radically different perspectives on religion. What he chose to pay attention to in 1930 was religion as a threat to the humanistic society he propagated, whereas in 1966 he points out how religion is a tool by which to reach that utopia.

In the former case, he needed to concentrate on how the dogma was interpreted and utilized by the rulers of society, but in the latter, he remains with theological speculations regardless of their use in society through history.

As for Christianity, he concludes that the original ideas of it were good, but they were corrupted when put to use in society. For Judaism, which has had far less influence on societies around the world, he just settles with the first part of the statement: the original ideas of it, as he interprets them, were good.

Judaism has never been put to the serious test that befell Christianity — the consequences of widespread success. Therefore, it is easy to claim Judaism's benefits, but not without the risk of turning it into an idol.

Considering Fromm's interest in social psychology and its dynamics, it is disappointing that he does not even try to speculate on what kind of corruption the Old Testament dogma as he understands it would risk if applied on a grander scale in society.

When he was 41 years old, Fromm released the book he may be most famous for: *Escape from Freedom*, discussed earlier. There he examined the Old Testament's account of the fall, when Adam and Eve bit the forbidden fruit and were expelled from the Garden of Eden. Seeing this as the first act of freedom, when man truly becomes man, he admitted that this was not the Bible's interpretation of the event. He used it as a symbolic starting point for his discussion about the need for humankind to become independent of a deity as well as of other authorities.

This was a very different take on the Bible from that of *You Shall Be as Gods*, 25 years later. In the previous book, he did not in any way claim that his interpretation of the Bible was identical to its original meaning or God's intention. On the contrary, he pointed out that he had his own twist on it.

God's worry and anger is just as evident in Fromm's text from 1941 as it is in Genesis. So is God's purpose. But in 1966 Fromm goes through all kinds of elaborate arguments to indicate that the Bible as well as its deity had a nobler intent than what meets the eye upon reading Genesis.

He points out that after creating man, God did not say that it was good, which he did with other creations of his. Thereby it was implied that man's creation was unfinished. God intended further development, which to Fromm can be nothing but the step towards freedom from the mother's womb of Paradise.[482] What might seem like an even more convincing argument is that the Bible never calls Adam's act a sin.[483] Well, it doesn't have to. God is quite clear about that in his response.

It is difficult to speculate on why Fromm would turn from the rebellious view towards the Bible when he was 41 to the apologist one when he was 66. It can't be as simple as the Swedish proverb states: "When the devil gets old, he gets religious."[484]

The transition of Fromm's thought and his reason for it may have been revealed already in the 1950 book *Psychoanalysis and Religion*, discussed earlier. In it, he complained about the materialism and superficiality he saw conquering society a few years after the end of Word War II. He argued for the religious perspective as a necessary antidote.

But he did so by altering the concept of religion to include spiritual doctrines and beliefs which do not contain any deities. Also, he made the distinction between authoritarian and humanistic religions, obviously propagating the latter. His use of the term religion was so odd that one has to wonder why he persisted with it. What he talked about is definitely closer to ethics, and his ideal could simply be described as compassion.

Still, his choice to reinterpret the principles of religion into

---

[482] Fromm, *You Shall Be as Gods*, p. 57.

[483] Ibid., p. 125.

[484] In Swedish, "När fan blir gammal blir han religiös." An old variation of it reads, "When the whore gets old, she gets godly." ("När horan blir gammal, blir hon gudfruktig.") Lars Rhodin, *Samling af swenska ordspråk*, Stockholm 1807, p. 101.

nodating his ideals, instead of finding another more fitting concept, would explain his development from exposing the flaws of the Bible into making it a companion, an ally, in 1966. Also in this respect, his development approached that of Carl G. Jung.

The Freudian Who Would Be a Jungian

The remaining conundrum with Erich Fromm is why he didn't become a Jungian. Though partially critical of Freud's theories, Fromm held him high all through his life.

On the year of his death in 1980, Fromm's book *Greatness and Limitations of Freud's Thought* was published. Already in the first sentence of the preface, he speaks of "the extraordinary significance of Freud's psychoanalytic discoveries" and compares it to the words in John 8:32: "And the truth shall make you free."[485] That is praise in absurdum.

Jung is mentioned only five times, and not a single one of his many books is listed in the bibliography — although Fromm had definitely read several of them. His first mention of Jung is an interesting combination of praise and dismissal. Considering Freud's insistence on sexuality as the root of all drives, he writes:

> *It was Jung who later cut loose from this connection, and in this respect made, as I see it, a truly valuable addition to Freud's thought.*[486]

Seeing Jung's standpoint as merely an addition to Freud's thought is both an insult and incorrect. Jung opposed Freud on this and other issues, unable to change Freud's mind. It was not a question of adding to Freud's theory, since he didn't allow any deviation from it. Fromm cannot have been unaware of this. He hid his disrespect for Jung inside a compliment.

[485] Erich Fromm, *Greatness and Limitations of Freud's Thought*, 1980, p. ix.
[486] Ibid., pp. 5f.

That is particularly disappointing coming from a man so occupied in his writing with ethics. I see no other explanation than that he found Jung a competitor with theories much like his own. Maybe he was bitter about having followed Freud for so long, instead of turning his attention to Jung, whose thoughts definitely fitted his own speculations much better?

Literature

Abraham, Karl:
Dreams and Myths: A Study in Race Psychology, transl. William A. White, New York 1913 (originally published in German 1909).

Alexander, Franz & Eisenstein, Samuel & Grotjahn, Martin:
Psychoanalytic Pioneers, New York 1966.

Anderson, Rasmus B. (transl.):
The Younger Edda, Chicago 1880.

Aristotle:
Poetics, transl. Stephen Halliwell, London 1999.

Breuer, Josef & Freud, Sigmund:
Studies in Hysteria, transl. A. A. Brill, New York 1936 (originally published in German 1895).

Brown, Paula & Tuzin, Donald F. (ed.)
The Ethnography of Cannibalism, Washington D.C. 1983.

Budge, E. A. Wallis:
The Book of the Dead: The Papyrus of Ani, New York 1967.
The Gods of the Egyptians: Studies in Egyptian Mythology, vol. 1 and 2, London 1904.

Campbell, Joseph:
The Hero with a Thousand Faces, Princeton 1968 (first edition 1949).

Darwin, Charles:
The Variation of Animals and Plant under Domestication, vol. 2, 2nd edition, London 1875.

da Vinci, Leonardo:
The Notebooks of Leonardo da Vinci, transl. Edward MacCurdy, New York 1955 (first published in 1939).

Deutsch, Helene:

A Psychoanalytic Study of the Myth of Dionysus and Apollo: Two Variants of the Son-Mother Relationship, New York 1969.

Diogenes Laertius:

Lives of Eminent Philosophers, vol. 1 and 2, transl. R. D. Hicks, London 1925.

Eeden, Frederik van:

"A Study of Dreams," *Proceedings of the Society for Psychical Research*, vol. 26, Glasgow 1913.

Eliade, Mircea:

From Primitives to Zen: A Thematic Sourcebook of the History of Religions, New York 1967.

The Myth of the Eternal Return, transl. Willard R. Trask, New York 1954 (originally published in 1949). The 1959 edition was renamed *Cosmos and History: The Myth of the Eternal Return*, and the 1965 edition *The Myth of the Eternal Return or, Cosmos and History*.

The Quest: History and Meaning in Religion, Chicago 1969.

Ferenczi, Sándor:

Thalassa: A Theory of Genitality, transl. Henry Alden Bunker, New York 1938 (originally published in German 1924).

Frazer, James G.:

The Fear of the Dead in Primitive Religion, London 1933.

The Golden Bough: A Study in Comparative Religion, vol. 1 and 2, London 1890.

The Golden Bough: A Study of Magic and Religion, abridged edition, New York 1922.

Freeman, Kathleen:

The Pre-Socratic Philosophers, Oxford 1946.

Freud, Sigmund:

An Autobiographical Study, transl. James Strachey, London 1935 (originally published in 1925).

Civilization and Its Discontents (*Das Unbehagen in der Kultur, 1930*), transl. Joan Riviere, London 1930.

Civilization and Its Discontents, transl. James Strachey, New York 1962.

Das Unbehagen in der Kultur, Wien 1930.

Inhibitions, Symptoms and Anxiety, transl. Alix Strachey, London 1936 (originally published in German 1926).

Leonardo da Vinci: A Psychosexual Study of an Infantile Reminiscence, transl. A. A. Brill, New York 1916.

"L'Hérédité et l'étiologie des névroses," *Revue neurologique*, volume 4 (6), Paris, 1896.

Moses and Monotheism, transl. Katherine Jones, Letchworth 1939 (originally published in German the same year as *Der Mann Moses und die monotheistische Religion*).

Sexuality and the Psychology of Love, New York 1963.

The Future of an Illusion, transl. James Strachey, New York 1961 (originally published in German 1927).

The History of the Psychoanalytic Movement, transl. A. A. Brill, New York 1917 (originally published in German 1914).

The Interpretation of Dreams, transl. A. A. Brill, New York 1913 (originally published in German 1899).

Totem and Taboo, transl. A. A. Brill, New York 1918 (originally published in German 1913).

Freud, Sigmund & Rank, Otto:

The Letters of Sigmund Freud and Otto Rank: Inside Psychoanalysis, edited by E. James Lieberman and Robert Kramer, Baltimore 2012.

Fromm, Erich:

Escape from Freedom, New York 1976 (originally published in German 1941).

Greatness and Limitations of Freud's Thought, 1980.

Psychoanalysis and Religion, New Haven 1967.

The Dogma of Christ, and Other Essays on Religion, Psychology, and Culture, Greenwich Connecticut 1963.

The Forgotten Language: An Introduction to the Understanding of Dreams, Fairy Tales and Myths, New York 1951.

You Shall Be as Gods: A Radical Interpretation of the Old Testament and Its Tradition, Greenwich 1966.

Gennep, Arnold van:

The Rites of Passage, Chicago 1960 (originally published in French 1909).

George, Andrew (transl.):
The Epic of Gilgamesh, London 1999.

Grosskurth, Phyllis:
The Secret Ring: Freud's Inner Circle and the Politics of Psychoanalysis, Reading 1991.

Hastings, James, ed.:
Encyclopædia of Religion and Ethics, 13 vols., Edinburgh 1908-1927.

Hertwig, Oscar:
"Beiträge zur Kenntniss der Bildung, Befruchtung und Theilung des thierischen Eies," *Morphologisches Jahrbuch,* vol. 1, Leipzig 1876.

Hesiod:
Theogony, transl. Glenn W. Most, Loeb 57, Cambridge Massachusetts 2006.

Jones, Ernest:
Essays in Applied Psycho-Analysis, London 1923.

Jung, Carl G.:
Collected Papers on Analytical Psychology, ed. Constance E. Long, London 1916, and 2nd edition, New York 1917.

Contributions to Analytical Psychology, transl. H. G and C. F. Baynes, London 1928.

Psychological Types or The Psychology of Individuation, transl. H. Godwin Baynes, London 1923.

Psychology of the Unconscious, transl. Beatrice M. Hinkle, New York 1916 (originally published in German 1912 as *Wandlungen und Symbole der Libido*).

The Psychology of the Transference, New York 1998 (originally published in German 1946).

The Theory of Psychoanalysis, New York 1915 (originally published in German 1913 as *Versuch einer Darstellung der psychoanalytischen*).

Jung, Carl G. & Kerényi, Károly:
On a Science of Mythology: The Myth of the Divine Child and the Mysteries of Eleusis, transl. R. F. C. Hull, New York 1949 (originally published in 1942).

Jung, Carl G. & Riklin, Franz:
"Experimentelle Untersuchungen über Assoziationen Gesunder," *Journal für Psychologie und Neurologie*, Band III, Heft 5, 1904.

Koestler, Arthur:
The Act of Creation, New York 1964.

Kroeber, A. L.:
"Totem and Taboo: An Ethnologic Psychoanalysis," *American Anthropologist*, vol. 22, 1920.

Lang, Andrew:
Myth, Ritual & Religion, vol. 1 and 2, London 1887.

Lang, Andrew & Atkinson, James Jasper:
Social Origins & Primal Law, London 1903.

Legge, James:
The Sacred Books of China: The Texts of Taoism, part 1, Oxford 1891.

Liddell, Henry George & Scott, Robert:
An Intermediate Greek-English Lexicon, Oxford 1889.

Long, John:
Voyages and Travels of an Indian Interpreter and Trader, London 1791.

Marinelli, Lydia & Mayer, Andreas:
Dreaming by the book: Freud's interpretation of dreams and the history of the psychoanalytic movement, transl. Susan Fairfield, New York 2003 (originally published in German 2002).

Mason, J. Moussaieff:
The Oceanic Feeling: The Origins of Religious Sentiment in Ancient India, Dordrecht 1980, p. 34.

Meng, Heinrich & Freud, Ernst L. (ed.):
Psychoanalysis and Faith. The Letters of Sigmund Freud and Oskar Pfister, transl. Eric Mosbacher, New York 1963.

Merkur, Dan:
Psychoanalytic Approaches to Myth: Freud and the Freudians, New York 2005.

Müller, Max:
Lectures on the Science of Language, London 1861.

Nygren, Anders:
Agape and Eros, transl. Philip S. Watson, Philadelphia 1953 (originally published in Swedish as *Den kristna kärlekstanken genom tiderna. Eros och Agape*, part I 1930 and part II 1936).

Pfister, Oscar:
Christianity and Fear: A Study in History and in the Psychology and Hygiene of Religion, transl. W. H. Johnston, London 1948 (originally published in German 1944).

Some Applications of Psycho-Analysis, unnamed translator, London 1923 (originally published in German 1920 and 1921).

"The Illusion of a Future: A Friendly Disagreement with Prof. Sigmund Freud," transl. Susan Abrams & Tom Taylor, ed. Paul Roazen, *The International Journal of Psycho-Analysis*, vol. 74 issue 3, London 1993 (originally published in German 1928).

The Psychoanalytic Method, transl. Charles Rockwell Payne, New York 1917 (originally published in German 1913).

Plato:
The Republic, transl. Paul Shorey, vol. 2, London 1942.

Poe, Edgar Allan:
The Complete Poems of Edgar Allan Poe, Boston 1917.

Rank, Otto:
The Double: A Psychoanalytic Study, transl. Harry Tucker jr., New York 1979 (originally published in German 1925).

The Myth of the Birth of the Hero: A Psychological Interpretation of Mythology, transl. F. Robbins and Smith Ely Jelliffe, New York 1914 (originally published in German 1909).

The Trauma of Birth, London 1929 (originally published in German 1924).

Read, John:
From Alchemy to Chemistry, New York 1995.

Reik, Theodor:
Ritual: Psycho-Analytic Studies, transl. Douglas Bryan, London 1931 (originally published in German 1928).

Rhodin, Lars:
Samling af swenska ordspråk, Stockholm 1807.

Riklin, Franz:
Wishfulfillment and Symbolism in Fairy Tales, transl. Wm. A. White, New York 1915 (originally published in German 1908).

Róheim, Géza:
"Primitive Man and Environment," *The International Journal of Psycho-Analysis*, volume II:2, 1921.

The Eternal Ones of the Dream: A Psychoanalytic Interpretation of Australian Myth and Ritual, New York 1945.

The Panic of the Gods and Other Essays, New York 1972.

Sales, François de:
Œuvres complètes : Lettres, vol. 1, Paris 1821.

Schoonheten, Anna Bentinck van:
Karl Abraham: Life and Work, a Biography, transl. Liz Waters, New York 2018.

Sellin, Ernst:
Mose und seine Bedeutung für die israelitisch-jüdische Religionsgeschichte, Leipzig 1922.

Shakespeare, William:
The Complete Works of William Shakespeare, London 1973.

Strindberg, August:
Plays by August Strindberg, transl. Edwin Björkman, New York 1912.

Tylor, Edward B.:
Primitive Culture: Researches into the Development of Mythology, Philosophy, Religion, Art, and Custom, vol. 1 and 2, London 1871.

Researches Into the Early History of Mankind and the Development of Civilization, London 1865.

Web Sources

Alvarez, Sara et al.:

"Male-directed infanticide in spider monkeys," *Primates*, volume 56:2, 2015, p. 173 (springer.com).

Dorsey, John M.:

An American Psychiatrist in Vienna, 1935-1937, and His Sigmund Freud, Detroit 1976. (web.archive.org/web/20070626155735/http://www.freud.org.uk/fmfaq.htm).

Dunham, Will:

"Infanticide common among adult males in many mammal species," *Reuters*, November 13, 2014 (reuters.com).

Jabr, Ferris:

"Study of Fetal Perception Takes Off," *scientificamerican.com*, 2015.

O'Toole, Garson:

"Genius Is One Percent Inspiration, Ninety-Nine Percent Perspiration," quoteinvestigator.com/2012/12/14/genius-ratio/.

Wikipedia:

"Scopes Trial."

www.ingramcontent.com/pod-product-compliance
Lightning Source LLC
LaVergne TN
LVHW091533070526
838199LV00001B/47